SUMMERS IN A TENT

recollections from a childhood

SUMMERS IN A TENT

recollections from a childhood

To the memory of

Elna and Gordon Bunker

TABLE OF CONTENTS

SUMMERS IN A TENT

recollections from a childhood

x

FOREWORD

For my sister Vic and me, spending the entirety of our childhood summers living in a tent by a lake made quite an impact on our lives.

Recently I bought a new ultra lightweight backpacking tent and was excited in anticipation of all those times and adventures yet to happen in it. On the way home from the store I got thinking about all my experiences in tents and decided to write this book. In an email to Vic I informed her about starting this project. She replied this was great news and filled me in on her day. She's a consulting archeologist: "I've put in a full field day, and enjoyed every minute - back out there tomorrow - feels good." She never says anything like this when she's writing a report.

We are two peas from the same pod. I had an office job once. The same room, desk, canned music and the same fluorescent lighting, every day. It almost did me in.

SUMMERS IN A TENT

Every Saturday morning at 11 o'clock, air raid sirens sing their haunting distress call in my home town of Concord, New Hampshire. Ostensibly this is to be sure the system is functioning properly, but in retrospect my hunch is it is more a reminder for all of us to be fearful. Of what exactly is a mystery, but we're deep in a "Cold War."

Springtime is upon us, trees are budding, and my folks are figuring out how to go camping. Not for a weekend or a week, but for the entire summer. Who's idea this was is unknown, but it's probably mom's. At the time I am five, so none of this is on my little screen until one day, right around the end of school my mother announces to my sister and me, "We're going to the lake for the summer. What do you think of that?" She is standing there in the kitchen on crutches, which seems to make no difference. The previous winter mom was skiing and got hit from behind. Whoever hit her didn't stop, didn't even slow down. The result was a crushed right ankle that is still in a cast and promises to remain so well into summer.

Vic is ten, so she is the one to ask the questions, the smart ones at least. More or less I'm off in my own little world. "Lake? What Lake?" she asks. We must present a formidable duo, both being red heads, being very close as friends and if I may say so, smart.

"Lake Wentworth. You know, the one we go past when we take the long way to Auntie's," mom answers.

"Where will we stay?" asks Vic. "Will there be snakes?" Her cherubic little face is a picture of concern. Ever since the story about a timber rattler being killed on Cotton Mountain (right behind Auntie's), well, life has never been the same. Seeing how New Hampshire is frozen solid at least half the year, you rarely see snakes and that makes them especially scary. Eleven o'clock comes around and the siren goes off: Rrr…whheeeee… whaaaaa, Rrr… wheeeee… whaaaaa…

And it generally freaks us all out. I cover my ears. "I hate that thing!" I say. Vic and I look at each other, then at mom and wait for it to quiet down. Finally, the thing gives its last whaaaaa.

Mom blusters and takes a deep breath, "We're going camping in a tent. And no. There will not be any snakes. No snakes."

Vic and I both know there's no way anyone can be so certain. "What about water moccasins?" asks Vic. She's just starting to get revved up. "Mom? What about water moccasins?" she repeats before mom has a chance to respond.

"You just don't need to worry about snakes," mom says. "Stop worrying about them. That timber rattler got killed on Cotton Mountain thirty years ago and no one's seen one since." And she very cleverly changes the subject to one she knows will be less contentious. "What do you two want for lunch?" she asks.

"Spaghetti-O's!" I scream.

"Those are gross," says Vic. It took me about fifteen years, but eventually I happened to read the ingredients on a can of them one day and came to the conclusion she was right. That can of Spaghetti-O's was my last.

"No they're not," I say, then look at mom. "Are they?"

"No dear, they're not," she says, but not very convincingly. She shoots my sister a look which says, "Your brother likes Spaghetti-O's and therefore he will eat them, and please keep in mind all I have to do is open a can which is of tremendous value." And then she asks my sister, "Victoria, what would you like for lunch?"

Vic considers her mental checklist of options. "An egg salad sandwich, please."

"And so you shall have," says mom. Vic and I sit at the kitchen table. The cat saunters in and heads for his bowls. He gives his food a sniff, backs away from it and dejectedly looks up at mom. Seeing she is paying no attention to him, he gets his nose into it and eats. We're talking Calo Cat Food. Think tan meat packing byproduct marshmallow fluff in a can that smells really bad. Why the poor cat lasted as long as he did eating this crap I don't know.

"Are we going to bring Tippy camping with us?" asks Vic.

The Spaghetti-O's are now a bubbling lava pit in the Club Aluminum pan on the stove. Little droplets of the pasty tomato sauce rocket into space and spatter on the white porcelain range top. A flock of evening grosbeaks are cleaning out the feeder. Mom pauses in the middle of peeling hard boiled eggs and stares out the window over the sink. She probably hadn't thought through the implications of bringing the cat, but she is now. "Yes dear, of course," she answers. The cat looks up from his Calo and stares at mom. Or maybe he's looking at the grosbeaks, thinking one of those might taste pretty good right about now.

I get my Spaghetti-O's, with the little meatballs floating around, and Vic gets her egg salad sandwich: two slabs of First National white bread with egg salad and a few pale green, translucent leaves of iceberg lettuce peeking out around the perimeter. Mom puts a dish of green olives stuffed with pimento on the table and Vic and I grab at them and hold them up to our eyes and roll them around all googly like. We giggle and snicker. "Now you two," mom says. "Don't play with your food." She pours herself another cup of coffee.

. . .

Spring turns to summer, the black flies are out in force and it's getting hot which also means it's getting ungodly humid. New Hampshire is a land of extremes; frigid winters, blistering summers and rugged landscape. But no matter what the season or where you go one thing is constant, it's humid. By the end of May, every kid in the known universe is ready to get out of school. The teachers have the windows opened wide and tall, and turn off the lights. At some point they give up trying to teach. They gaze out upon their gathered flock and all of them look limp, dissociative and despondent. And sweaty. "Class, why don't we fold our arms on our desks and put our heads down for a rest?" they suggest, and we gladly collapse. With the kids thus quiet the teachers turn their attention to the magazines... *Better Homes and Gardens, McCalls, Popular Mechanics*, they'd rather be looking at anyway.

Meanwhile, mom and dad are getting the whole camping shebang ready to go. One hot Saturday afternoon we all get in the Buick and go to Sears to buy a tent. The sporting goods department is downstairs which is a good thing because it's cooler down there. They don't have enough floor space to display the actual tents, so they have little scale models set up on squares of plywood. The three room Ted Williams looks like the one for us. A bedroom on each end, a family room in the middle and an awning out front. It's royal blue. The models have real screen in the windows, and teeny zippers and little aluminum poles and the plywood is coated with bright green flocking to look like grass. Dad must wonder why our lawn never looks this good. I do my best to pretend I'm about three inches tall, and conclude this one ought to be plenty big enough. The clerk rings up the sale and tells us he'll get one from stock and meet us at the loading dock out back. We eagerly head out, and dad backs the Buick up to the dock and out comes the clerk, sweating and struggling with a giant box held together with metal strapping, teetering on a hand truck. He loses control of it and partly saves it by giving it a shove and WHAM! The towering box falls over onto the cement, kicking up a cloud of dust and sand and bits of trash. We all jump back, coughing and waving our hands around. That was a close one. Dad and the clerk just barely muscle the thing into the trunk of the idling car, the springs settle almost to bottom. Good thing we brought the Buick. This load would have broken Dad's Peugeot in two. Mom gets behind the wheel, this is after all, her car, and sputters, "Bunk... you didn't turn on the air!" This is our first car with air conditioning and by God, she is going to use it. She fiddles with the controls and in a minute Vic and I are wishing we brought sweaters.

Vic and I, being the little smarty-pants we were (still are), would pick on mom when she said anything about, "turning on the air." The whole planet is surrounded by air we would argue. It's not something you "turn on." This was only one of many ways we would get her goat.

Dad gets in, drenched with sweat and looking like a heart attack in search of a place to happen. Both mom and dad smoke cigarettes and drink. Too much. He's a quiet type and doesn't say anything about "the air," but by the time we get to Haggett's Sport Shop two blocks down the street his teeth are chattering.

At Haggett's, while mom and dad are checking out Coleman stoves and lanterns, I stay close, this is a new and foreign world to me. Guns and fishing poles and strange things. And they have dead animal heads and big fish hanging from the walls, that's pretty weird, why would you want dead animal heads and big fish hanging around? I point to one of the fish, and ask, "Mom, why don't they smell bad?"

"They're stuffed," she replies. She's trying to figure out if we need a two or three burner stove. The three burner is a monster.

This answer doesn't make sense so I inquire further, "Like the turkey?"

"No, Gordon... hold on a moment," she says. She kneels down. "The turkey we stuff with good things to eat and then roast it in the oven. The fish up there, after the fisherman caught it he took it to a taxidermist..." I look at my mom, clearly wondering who or what a taxidermist is, and she says, "this is a person who preserves fish and animals so they don't smell bad and can be put on display, like these."

Preserves. I'm going to think about this. "Thanks mom," I say. Why would you want to preserve a fish instead of eat it? I look up at the fish again. "What do they stuff them with?" I ask.

"I don't know," says mom, just a wee bit exasperated. "Ask your father."

Having decided on a two burner stove and a lantern, and the biggest cooler known to mankind, we get out of there. When

8

we get home my dad doesn't know what to do with the tent. He'd be hard-pressed to get it out of the car on his own, but he doesn't want to leave all that weight in the trunk for two weeks. He calls our neighbor, Mr. G., who is right over to help. Mr. G. has a pot belly and beady eyes and smells funny. His son Dicky is with him and he's my best friend. My dad and Mr. G. get the tent out of the trunk and lean it in the corner of the garage. My dad looks at his watch. "The sun's over the yard arm, Dick. Care for a cold one?" Mr. G's face lights up and he replies in the affirmative. Dad disappears into the house and comes out with two bottles of Carling Black Label which are already sweating as much as he is. He and Mr. G. stand there and drink the beers and smack their lips in satisfaction and talk about boring grown-up things. This is a good time for Dicky and me to play trucks in the sand pile behind the garage.

We are so close to summer vacation. Every child and teacher in the public school system languishes in the hot and sticky classrooms. Everyone is cranky, there's just so much napping we can do at our desks. Every teacher fritters away the hours, fantasizing behind their magazines, fantasizing about how nice three months of not having to deal with these rooms full of little disciplinary problems will be. They, like the rest of us, simply want to get the heck out of here. Meanwhile, all the parents are wondering anxiously what they're going to do their kids on their hands 24/7 for those same three months.

Not our parents. They know what they are going to do... let us run around like wild banshees every day, and swim and get sunburned and generally tire ourselves to the point of exhaustion so by the end of each day we will literally collapse into our sleeping bags and not a peep will be heard until next morning. Pretty clever. Mom is maybe wondering how this will all go with her being on crutches, but if ever there is a woman with verve for life, and the ability to toss obstacles aside, she is it.

To keep me occupied the final week at home, mom puts me to work sticking S&H Green Stamps into books. She gets the stamps at the First National. The checkers have these machines with dials on them a lot like telephones and depending on the order's total, they dial out so many stamps in different denominations. No one in our family especially likes sticking all these things in the books, but I've cut a deal with mom for a piece of the action - there's a nautical theme table lamp in the catalog I have my eye on for my bedroom. I sit at the table for what seems like forever with a pile of stamps and the books and a wet sponge on a plate. Part of it is figuring out how many singles, fives, tens or fifties it will take to fill a page. The fifty is one stamp to a page so that's a no-brainer, and boy I like those fifties. My fingers turn green from the dye on the stamps, but I am on a mission. These books we will redeem for sleeping bags, and I've already picked mine out. It's chocolate brown canvas on the outside and red flannel on the inside with a hunt scene print. It's a picture of a man and a dog and a pheasant. The man stands in a thicket of grasses and holds up a shotgun, the dog is on point and if I didn't know any better it's smiling. It's cool when dogs smile. The plump pheasant is most definitely not smiling. He's on the wing, flapping madly, trying his darnedest to get away from the guy with the gun, pronto, asap, like now! without getting blown to smithereens. I look at the scene and wonder what happens next.

. . .

Finally the big day, the biggest day, the only one out of a hundred eighty in school that ever really matters comes. The last day. Wow, tomorrow every kid will wake up and NOT have to go to school. Three months of freedom stretch before us, a veritable eternity. Every kid is jubilant walking home. Skipping home. Shouting the things you wanted to say to kids you don't especially like, knowing there are three months for them to forget about it before you have to face them again. When I get home that afternoon I take my shoes off and little do I know, this marks the beginning of summers, each without wearing shoes, for the next ten years. Entire summers. I love being barefoot, just love it. No shoes for three months. Freedom!

Vic gets home right about the same time, and Mom takes a pitcher of Kool-Aid from the fridge and pours big glasses full for us. It's brilliant green, full of sugar and 100% artificial lime flavor, and nothing could be better.

We load the Buick. This is a 1960 Electra 225, a beast with more steel in the hood than is found in an entire Hyundai. It's painted a handsome dark metallic green and has a white roof. Loading the car takes days, and on the eve of our departure dad takes off on an Air Force Reserve mission to some far flung place. He is a pilot and flies big transport aircraft. Feeling, with some accuracy she played second fiddle to airplanes mom once sniffed, "If your father could have had sex with an airplane, he would have married one!" By the time we have all our junk in the car there is barely room for the three of us. Four, including the cat. But off we go, mom steady at the helm, the car creaks and groans under the load. The springs in the back have to be bottomed out. The bill of lading reads: tent, stove, lantern, fuel, cooler (fully stocked), portable liquor cabinet (also fully stocked), cots, sleeping bags, folding chairs, hibachi, charcoal briquettes, lighter fluid, thunderjug (with Esso bumper sticker reading "A Chicken

In Every Pot - A Tiger In Every Tank"), folding table, picnic basket, paper plates, plastic cups, silverware, dish tub, dish soap, duffels of clothes, Parcheesi board, Ouija board (useful for weather forecasts, foretelling of future events and unlocking padlocks on the mysterious past), coloring books, crayons, books to read, cat food, can opener, pots and pans and etc. & etc.. And a few more etcetera's for good measure.

Crammed into the front seat, we pull out of the driveway and take one last look at the house. Mom's flower gardens are looking good; tulips and croci are long passed, but the phlox petunias and daisies are coming in strong. She loves her gardens and they're doing nicely and over the next three months in her absence they'll turn into jungle thickets. If our house is ever featured in a tour of gardens it will be as an example of what not to do. By the end of the driveway, and it is by no means a long one, Tippy starts yowling. So far, getting in the car means only one thing to him: he is going to the vet. Even though we think the vet is a nice person, he does not. After many years of going to the lake the poor cat never did get it. Or maybe he did, and it was in it's own right something worth yowling about. Whatever the case, except for brief interludes of panting, he keeps it up all the way to Wolfeboro.

It's puzzling how certain inventions, given their obvious benefits to humankind no matter what time period we're talking about, haven't always existed. Take for example the cat carrier. In 1963 there simply is no such thing. Tippy is all over the place, and in his trauma eventually decides to settle in among mom's feet and the car's pedals. So now, before applying the brakes mom has to nudge Tippy out of the way. Just another pesky complication added to the fact there is a cast on her right foot that goes up to her knee. Oh, the perils we survive.

Of course we have the "air" blasting and the windows are closed. We cross the Merrimack River and are reminded the "air" does nothing to filter out the stink. There is at this time no such thing as sewage treatment and the river is nothing more than a moving cesspool. It stinks even in winter, but in summer it is pure nastiness! Crossing the river marks our exodus from Concord, a good thing. Somewhere along the shortcut through Chichester we get behind a bus. This, like most roads in New Hampshire is a narrow roller coaster, put down in the days before big earth moving equipment, so it follows the terrain rather than plow through it. Must be quite a ride in a bus. Giant billowing clouds of sooty diesel exhaust loom behind it. Being the kid I am, I rather enjoy the smell of it, and so to better get its aroma I open the window and stick my head out into the clouds. FYI, I've since given up my exhaust sniffing habit.

"Gordon! Close the window or the cat will get out!" yells mom.

"But mom, I like the smell of the bus," I reply. Vic is sitting in the middle. She smartly decides to keep out of this one. Either that, or she is focusing on not getting car sick. I put the window back up so it is open only a little bit. Instead of getting my entire head out in the flow, it will have to suffice to stick my nose out the opening. Satisfied after a good long whiff, I withdraw my nose from the airstream and close the window.

"That can't be good for you, dear," says mom.

I shrug my shoulders. "But I like it," I say.

"You're such a weirdo," says Vic.

"Mom, can we go to The Scandinavian Gift Shop?" I ask.

"I'm afraid not," she says. "It wouldn't be fair to Tippy leaving him in the car."

I am bummed. I love this place, run by a kindly little old Swedish lady in the front of her home. The place is packed to the gills with all manner of cool Swedish craft items. Made by elves. I am already amassing a collection of brightly painted carved wooden horses. But today we are on a mission. Get to the lake intact, with enough of the day left to pitch the tent and get to something resembling settled. By some set of minor miracles we make it to Wolfeboro, it's a lot like going to Auntie Tora's but we take the lake road, and as advertised there is the plywood sign just beyond the bridge over Wiley Brook. It has weeds growing up around it and is crudely painted in red letters on a white background, proclaiming, "Robies Family Campground."

Mom wheels the great listing Buick in on the dirt road and we are immediately transported into a cool shady world of narrow dirt tracks through a forest of towering pine trees. The tracks are crisscrossed with thick woody roots and the car humps and bumps over them. It's kinda fun. Through the trees, we get our first glimpses of Lake Wentworth, cool rippling blue water stretching out, with the Belknap Mountains hovering in the background. A hand painted sign on a spindly post that's almost tipping over tells us to, "Check In At Office" and right there, above the door of a haphazardly built but well kept camp hangs an even smaller sign, "Office." This must be the place. Before we can get out of the car, a smiling Elbridge Robie comes tottering out to greet us. He stops, and while he doesn't especially look like a nervous type, he has a funny way of rocking his weight from foot to foot. Maybe his feet hurt.

We spill out of the Buick. "Keep the cat in the car!" exclaims mom, but there's no way. Cats are remarkably agile and quick. And they have claws. Tippy lunges from the car, gets about ten feet away and suddenly realizes he's not in Kansas anymore. Nor is he at the vet's. He stops dead in his tracks, looks around and then at us and meows. We're all looking at him in collective horror that we've just lost him to the big piney woods. He, however, sits down and licks his paw, perfectly relaxed as though this is what he had in mind all along.

Mr. Robie welcomes us in a soft spoken, friendly way. Mom grew up on Cotton Mountain, so she and Robie are already well acquainted and they have a good time yammering away. Just like old home week. Vic goes after the cat and I listen to Mr. Robie. Not what he's saying, but how he's saying it. He's an Old Timer and has the New Hampsha accent.

Miraculously Vic apprehends Tippy, or maybe he decided it's a good idea to stick with his humans. When we get back in the car, I blurt out, "Mr. Robie talks funny." Mom looks at me with fire in her eyes and shushes me. She quickly pulls her door closed. "Let's not have Mr. Robie hear you say that," she hisses.

. . .

My grandparents Elsa and Arvid Nelson, a.k.a. Barb and Pamp, help Mr. Robie run the place and are staying in a ramshackle cottage near the water. Mom pilots the Buick very slowly over the bumps and through the trees to our site next to the cottage, all the while hoping we don't get stuck in the sand. We quickly see we have scored *the* site in the whole campground. We'll be tucked in the trees on the side of the cove, with a sandy beach on one side and a broad view to the lake on the other. We get out of the car, and Barb and Pamp are there to greet us. The air coming off the lake smells like water and is soft on the skin. It makes beautiful whooshing sounds passing through the trees.

Barb showers Vic and me with bosomy, dry powdery, "Oh, my darling angels," affection and lots of hugs and kisses, which always rather puts us off. But her heart's in the right place. Pamp on the other hand speaks in spoonerisms and shows his affection, if that's what you can call it, by pulling our hair. I have a fresh crew cut, so he's having a hard time of it but he's persistent. He can be mean in a weirdo kind of way. We take a tour of the cottage.

It's a typical summer cottage. The building is small, has no insulation and is built on footings, not a foundation. In other words, it's simple and it's not a house. The long side of Barb and Pamp's place faces the lake, and is all windows. They're simply hinged at the top and propped out with sticks. There are screens and the breeze coming off the water whispers through them, freely flowing inside. This is the main living space with a squeaky steel framed sofa bed at one end, a dining table and chairs in the middle and a china cabinet at the other end filled with campy dinnerware and glasses. The curved glass front is all wavy. In the back is the kitchen and bath and bedroom. There is no ceiling, so you can see the roof framing above. And this is it. The table is set for dinner for the five of us and the place smells of Barb's chili with a whiff of propane gas. There must be a leak somewhere. More than once as an adult I've tried to replicate Barb's chili, with just the right balance of heat, tanginess, and sweetness of onion and I've never been able to get it.

The day isn't going to last forever, and we have a tent to pitch. Mom moves the Buick closer to our site and opens the trunk and we start digging the contents out. In no time it looks like the circus is in town, which in a sense it is. We decide to take the tent out piece by piece, poles, lines, stakes, but sooner or later we're faced with the tent itself. It's a giant blue rolled up cotton canvas lump and it stinks like old used motor oil, probably the waterproofing applied to the fabric. And even on its own it weighs a ton. The canvas is the woven equivalent of quarter inch steel plate. Pamp gets Mr. Robie to help and I get in on it too, we all heave and ho and grunt but there's just no way to get ahold of it. Finally, we manage to get the lump out of the car and to the place we'll pitch it. We go over the ground for stones and twigs and things which might cause trouble if left under the tent, and toss them all aside. Mom has the instructions, all nine pages, and sits down on the picnic table bench with her casted leg outstretched, and starts calling the shots. If you want to know who your friends are, pitch a tent with them. And hopefully the wind isn't blowing a gale, or it's a downpour. With some head scratching, a few minor skirmishes and some trial and error we get the thing up. The front door faces the lake. Home sweet home, Vic and I get the thunderjug and cots and sleeping bags inside and the rest can wait. We're all whooped, and head back to Barb and Pamp's cottage. It's cocktail hour for the grown-ups and Coca Cola hour for Vic and me, and there's the smell of that chili. There's also Barb's aspic salad that will need to be consumed, politely, in small quantities we hope. This wiggly blob on the side of your plate, made from clarified horses hooves, with canned peas and maybe some tiny canned shrimp and other odd particles floating around in it is... disgusting! But three big spoons full of chili to one small forkful of aspic salad and things are going to be ok.

It's dark when we leave, and the batteries in the flashlight Pamp loans us could stand a change. The western horizon glows ever so slightly at the end of the long northern twilight, and through the inky silhouettes of the pines, the blue-black sky above is a blaze of stars. The tent is less than a hundred feet away, but it feels like wilderness to me. We tiptoe through the woods (mom hobbles, actually) by the flashlight's dimming orange glow, and by the time we get to the tent there's just enough light for Vic, under mom's tutelage, to first unzip the screen and then the door. Each has one central vertical zipper the entire height of the opening and at the threshold horizontal zippers span left and right. Standing there holding the flashlight I can hear the lake, small waves lapping against the shore.

Silently, Tippy appears from the darkness and scoots between our legs and into the tent. He's been out doing cat things, and smells like damp grass, and he's hungry. Meowing, he wriggles close around us, "Feed me!"

Mom asks, "Vicky, would you go out to the car and bring in the Coleman lantern?"

"By myself?" asks Vic.

"You'll be fine," says mom. "It's in a plastic bucket in the trunk. Here are the keys." Mom hands Vic a bundle of keys. "This one," she says, picking out the key for the trunk.

"But it's dark, and it's the woods," says Vic. "Can I take the flashlight?"

"Yes. Now just go ahead dear," says mom, "everything will be fine."

Vic picks up the flashlight and reluctantly steps out through the doorway. She pauses and scans the ground with the flashlight, probably looking for snakes. The coast is clear, she takes a tentative step and then vanishes. Mom and I are left sitting in the tent in pitch darkness. We can hear Vic open the trunk and then rummage around. In a moment she comes back with the green plastic bucket with the lantern and a box of matches in it, and sets it on the floor in front of mom.

"Thank you Wic*tor-i-a*," says mom. She likes adding a little Swedish accent when she's pleased. "Did you remember to close the trunk?"

"I couldn't reach it," says Vic.

"That's o.k., I'll take care of it after we get this going," says mom. Before dad left on his trip, he installed the mantles in the lantern. These are little booties of silk which get tied onto the ends of the gas feeder tubes and then burned to ash. He also filled the tank with white gas. "Vicky, would you shine the light on what I'm doing?"

"Sure mom," says Vic. Tippy still has dinner on his mind and is weaving around us. Vic bends over to give him a rub and the light beam goes astray.

"Shine the light here, dear," says mom. She lifts the lantern from the bucket and sets it on the picnic basket and then rapidly pumps up the tank with her thumb on the sliding pump thingy. Satisfied there's enough pressure, she takes a match from the box, opens the valve on the lantern - it hisses like a… no, never mind - strikes the match and puts the flame through the small hole in the lantern for this purpose, and poof!, sputter, wheeze… and miraculously it comes to life. The mantles ignite and glow and pulsate and when it gets settled, they burn a brilliant white. So bright you can't look at them. Mom sits back in her lawn chair, pretty pleased with herself. "How about that?" she asks.

Vic and I stand there in awe and smile.

Mom gets up from the chair, hobbles outside and with an authoritative wham closes the trunk of the Buick. She comes back inside. "We better close the door before all the bugs come in," she says. Already a few moths have found their way, flying madly around the light. It takes her some effort on her crutches - she's tired but she manages - to pull the high sections of the zippers down. Vic pulls them to the floor. "We'll leave the zippers at the bottom open for Tippy," she says. We figured the tent would be a little too cozy for a cat box. Tippy has given up on dinner and slinks out for a quick mouse.

Vic and I roll our sleeping bags out on our cots and then help mom with hers. She reminds us, "If you have to go potty in the night, that's what the thunderjug is for," pointing to the white enameled bucket with a cover. "And be careful to not kick it over!"

Mom gives us hugs and kisses good night. Her breath stinks like cigarettes and whiskey and even at this early age I am thinking I don't want her to kiss me. But the important thing is she loves us. Vic and I wriggle into our bags. The flannel is soft and fresh and warm, and mom closes the curtain giving us some darkness. "Sleep tight, and don't let the bed bugs bite," she says. The sound of the lantern is a comforting, waves lap the dark shore, and from the marsh bullfrogs start thumping. Thin shafts of light peek around the edges of the curtain and streak across the blue canvas walls. Mom rustles around and gets herself into her sleeping bag. Amazing, doing all of this with two kids while on crutches. She turns off the lantern, it sputters and goes out. Now it is still and dark, and in an instant I am asleep.

. . .

In the morning, patches of sunlight project onto the tent through the trees, the irregular shapes sway back and forth as a breeze slips through the branches. It's time to get up, so we get dressed in our bathing suits and in what will become a morning ritual unzip the screen and door, roll and tie them back. Powerful associations with the sound of a tent zipper are still with me. It gives me a feeling of being home more than any street or driveway or door.

Our eyes have adjusted to everything being blue, so our first peeks outside look red. The air is fresh, cool and crisp. It will be a while before my feet toughen up, so it's a distinct and mixed sensation to step outside into sand and pine needles.

Tippy is very interested in having breakfast, so we gather up a fresh can of Calo and the tools and accouterments of serving him a blob. He whips up into a frenzy during the process, the sound of the can opener, the smell of the stuff and finally the placing of the bowl on the tent floor. He doesn't play the "maybe if I hesitate I'll get something better," game, and dives in. "Make them wait long enough and they'll eat anything," says mom. She also says this when she serves certain dishes to us, shrimp wiggle being one of them. For the human breakfast we have an assortment pack of single serving boxes of cereal. My default choice is Fruit Loops and second pick is Frosted Flakes. Give me the sugar. The faces of the boxes are perforated, supposedly I should be able to open the package with my thumbnail like bulkhead doors, swing the flaps up and then with care do the same with the wax paper liner. All of this so mom has only to pour in some milk. After much effort, it works well enough and we three are sitting in folding lawn chairs under the front awning in the fresh air having breakfast. This is fun, eating your own cereal from your own little box. Then we have grapefruit halves, again I go for the sugar and keep sprinkling it on until there's a thick crust of the stuff, becoming translucent as it soaks up juice from the fruit. Amazing anyone in this culture gets to adulthood with any teeth left.

In the early years, Robie's offers what is called, "rustic camping." There are no utility hookups, there is no bathhouse and there is no flush toilet. There is a rickety old outhouse or two. A properly maintained outhouse is not such a bad thing, but then, I've never seen a properly maintained outhouse so I guess it's fair to say outhouses are disgusting. We however have the luxury of using Barb and Pamp's facilities in their cottage. Bathing options include a "PTA," as dad calls it (this is supposedly a military acronym for Pecker, Tits, and Asshole) in a washbasin of cold water, or if you're lucky warm water heated on the Coleman stove. We might also sneak into the lake after dark with a bar of soap, or for the deluxe spa treatment go to Auntie Tora's about five miles away for a genuine bath with genuine hot water in a genuine bathtub. Plus, Auntie wallpapered her bathroom with maps from National Geographic, so it's really cool to soak in the tub and gaze up and wonder about all those far away places. And for me, in time, having looked at a lot of Auntie's National Geographics with photographs of women without shirts holds particular interest, and so gazing at those maps I wonder how does one get to those far away places, anyway?

Now where was I? Oh right, we walk over to Barb and Pamp's, the place smells like coffee and mom's mood improves immediately. While she's having a cup or three with Barb, Vic and I take turns in the bathroom. The water that comes from the tap is drawn from the lake. We're not supposed to drink it but everyone does. The water is full of minerals and probably has more nutritional value than the Fruit Loops I just had for breakfast. It tastes good, if a little swampy. There's a tiny hot water tank in the corner that fills about a sink full before going cold. With our ablutions complete and our systems full of the stimulants of choice, we're ready to get on with the day.

"What are we going to do?" I ask mom.

"Let's go to the beach," she suggests.

Vic and I look at one another and I nod to mom. "O.K.," I say. "Where's the beach?"

"You'll see," she says. "Let's go back to the tent and get our towels and things." We gather up a sizeable pile of junk. Towels with garish colored images of palm trees and sailboats, plastic buckets and shovels, a chaise lounge for mom, the book she is reading, the bright green bottle of Sea & Ski suntan lotion. It isn't called sunblock because this stuff does nothing to prevent a burn. Mom is able to carry only a small bag with a few things in it, so Vic and I get the rest. The chaise we have to carry together, which turns into a herky-jerky struggle, not that we are fighting over it or anything, but we are basically very uncoordinated. The plastic webbing woven across the seat and back is scratchy. No way could you sit in one of these things with any skin exposed without first covering it with a towel. I make note mom is having a hard go of things with her crutch tips in the sand. This may be to my advantage at some point. Nonetheless, we make it to the beach and set up our goodies.

The beach wraps around a small cove Mr. Robie has carved into the shore of Wiley Brook. To one side a floating platform for bathing beauties to lay upon and display themselves, and for jumping into the water from, the intention being at least partly to splash a cool soothing spray onto the beauties for their comfort, of course. The platform is an old barge

Mr. Robie used in previous years to set navigation buoys in the lake. It's made from solid timbers saturated with creosote. Those were the days. EPA? We don't need any government official to tell us how to do things.

A rope is tied from the barge to a steel pipe pounded in the sand across the cove. It has old soccer balls strung on it as floats, and this is the limit we kids are not supposed to cross. One of our tricks is to push all the balls to one end of the rope and pretend we have no idea how this happened. Must be a prevailing wind. Then a grown-up would have to get in the water to space them out again. It's always fun to make grown-ups do things that annoy them.

The water is the color of tea. "Mom, why's the water that funny color?" asks Vic.

"It's from the pine trees, dear, called tannin," she replies.

"Is it ok?" asks Vic. "Are there any snakes?"

Mom looks up from *The Agony and the Ecstasy*, which somehow is an appropriate metaphor for something, maybe her life. "Now Victoria. The water is fine, the color won't hurt you. And with you and your brother splashing around, if there was any snake nearby, he'd be long gone," she says.

"But mom. We haven't started splashing around yet. So there could be snakes," says Vic, bless her little heart. Mom just looks at her. I'm already in the water, all the way up to my knees and I splash handfuls of water on Vic's back. She screams, turns and comes after me. I start splashing more water and she splashes back and before we know it we're both soaked.

It's early in the season and not too many kids have been in the water yet, so the bottom is all slimy. The slime squeezes up between my toes, and feels weird and funny. Like stepping barefoot in fresh dog poop, but a lot less gross. We're wearing our t-shirts to keep our pale and tender little fair skinned bodies from burning to a crisp this first time out. Now soaking wet, they are clammy and cling to us, and by the end of the day, everything not covered by the t-shirts is burned bright red, and it stings when you touch it.

Mr. Robie put a lot of effort into the place, but everything is a little backwoods engineered. Vic and I decide to explore around, and next to the beach in a flat sandy area Mr. Robie has built a shuffleboard court. The usual method would be to pour a concrete slab and make it very flat and very smooth and paint the appropriate numbers and triangles and things on it. But Mr. Robie decided to make a plywood deck on a platform of 2 x 4's and support it on stakes pounded into the sand. The thing isn't flat, and the edges of the sheets don't match and the plywood is delaminating in the weather and sun, and if you run around on it bare foot like we do, you are at risk of getting huge demonic splinters in your feet. Nasty! So we fool around with it, not that we would ever get the hang of it if it were completely functional. Soon we move on to other things like exploring in the tall grasses along the shore. The place is teaming with life, bright blue dragonflies zoom around, they fly any direction they want. Schools of minnows in the shallows see us coming and dart for cover, there are so many of them, so dense together they form a dark cloud moving in the water. Maybe we get in a fight and I'm throwing handfuls of gloppy wet sand and muck at Vic. Mom calls to us, "It's time for a nap you two."

We snap to attention. This is altogether too much fun to take a dreaded, boring nap. "Aww mom…" we whine. "Do we have to?"

"Yes," she says. "Come over here and let me rinse you off." We trudge over to her, where she's still ensconced on the chaise. "Why don't you fill your buckets with water?" she suggests. We tiptoe into the water and fill the buckets and bring them to mom. She then pours it over us, and it is wickedly cold on our hot sunburned little bodies. We shriek and jump around.

Back at the tent, we take off our t-shirts. What was covered is lily white, what was not is bright red. Mom slathers us down with Sea & Ski. It feels cold going on but eventually soothing. I lay on my sleeping bag. The tent is in deep shade now and all the windows are open. The breeze coming off the lake is soft with moisture and flows through the space. I can hear the sounds of other campers and of motorboats far out on the water, and have a feeling I'm part of it all. Vic is looking at a magazine, and Tippy hops up with her and curls up at the foot of her bag for a little nap of his own. Just the very end of his tail wags up and down, ever so slowly and then stops. It's easy to doze off.

. . .

Wolfeboro is "The Oldest Summer Resort in America," harking back to 1771 when Colonial Governor John Wentworth built a summer estate on Smith Pond which later was renamed Lake Wentworth. Somewhere off in the woods on the hill overlooking the east end of the lake is the cellar hole, which is all that's left of the place.

Way back then, the town of Wolfeboro didn't have a traffic light and by golly it still does not today. Whether or not to have one at the intersection of routes 109 and 28 is a highly political and hotly debated issue at town council meetings. Interesting, the things Wolfeboroites get passionate about, never mind there are a few more cars now and on a busy summer afternoon traffic gets backed up in all directions, sometimes for miles.

Some of the old timers turn into old farts - I know about this because it's happening to me - and they feel pushed by "progress" in a direction they don't particularly like. A few of them manage to connive their way into power, take moral high ground and by God, this is not the kind of town that has a traffic light. Nor are we those kind of people (meaning all liberals or people from Massachusetts) who condone such activity. So there. Eventually they do concede to a blinking red light, but only under threat of all our rioting in the streets.

Mom announces we are going into town and Vic and I immediately grab our sweaters. She looks at us like we've lost our minds. "You two, it has to be in the nineties. Why are you bringing sweaters?" she asks.

I pretend I'm having trouble getting on my flip-flops, essentially putting Vic on the spot, who stands there quietly for a moment, then says, "In case it gets cold." Mom must be wondering why was she blessed with two of the strangest creatures on earth posing as children.

So we go into town and get stuck in traffic, and it's 91 degrees and 98% humidity out there and mom has the air turned on and blasting. Vic and I already have our sweaters on, and I look at my feet which are turning blue and think long pants next time. Whether or not the trusty Buick can take this heat without boiling over is a grown up matter to which I am oblivious, but much to it's credit, it runs perfectly. Except one blistering day when mom and I drive to Logan airport to pick up Aunt Harriet and the old girl (the car, that is) gave up the ghost. But that debacle is outside the scope of this modest epistle.

We're in town to run errands and Vic and I are flip-flopping along behind mom. Today it's the Wolfeboro 5 And Dime (yes!), Hunter's Grocery "for a few items." Mom sputters vehemently about the prices at Hunter's, and will 'til her dying day. She just isn't able to let go of this one. The Yum-Yum Shop (yes again!) for fig squares for dad and raspberry squares for everyone else, the New Hampshire State Liquor Store (we go in there every time we go to town), and Moody's Ice House. There's a basin in the trunk for the block of ice.

The 5 And Dime is tucked into a small space below street level. It's bursting with bright colored cheap junk, so much that it spills out the door onto the sidewalk. Inside, there's just enough space to walk between the displays, and pathways are worn in the wood floor. Where everyone walks the finish is completely worn through, and then gradates to a dark chocolate brown mix of varnish and dirt close up to the displays. They have everything that's cool. Rubber lizards and chickens, kid size sunglasses, beach towels, umbrellas, you name it. My favorite is the pinwheel sparkler, a small mechanical toy you hold between your index and middle finger and then repeatedly press a plunger with your thumb. This spins a wheel with colored acetate windows that flash around past a sparkler, so it's all colors and sparks and commotion. Especially fun at night inside your sleeping bag. The lady at the register has jiggly arms and smells like baby powder and her hair is done up like a blue silver puff ball and she has a heart of gold and says to every snotty nosed little kid like me, "Thank you very much, Dee-ah," when we pay for our stuff.

Skipping down Main Street with my new pinwheel sparkler, I see a cowboy on a bucking bronco. He's on a license plate on a pickup truck. I stop and study it. The truck which probably started out dark blue, is now faded to a light silver blue. Trying to sound out the word on the license plate, I ask mom, "What's whyo-ming?"

She's gesturing to me to catch up with her and Vic. "Wyoming," she says, "is a place out west."

"What's out west?" I ask.

"Where we live is the east. West is another part of the country," she says, pointing toward Vermont. "Why are you so interested in the west?" she asks.

"That's where cowboys live, right?" I ask.

"Yes," she says.

"There's a picture of one on that truck. Come see," I say.

Mom reverses direction which is not an easy thing for her to do, and we look at the back end of the truck together. "Wyoming is a state far, far away. We'll look at a map when we get home," she says.

Across the street it's an entirely different scene at the Yum-Yum Shop. It's organized and bright and clean and everyone who works there wears a hair net, even the boys who wear permanent expressions of embarrassment. No matter when, no matter what, Vic and I are keenly interested in our next sugar rush. We are transfixed by the sights and smells of the delightful sweets in the glass front cases. We beg mom for everything in the store. I spot the sugar cookies, "Mom can I have some of..." and then the cupcakes get my attention, "... and some of these, and..."

Mom says to the young woman waiting on us who's trying to keep track of everything we're pointing at, "We'll have

29

four fig squares and eight raspberry squares please. You can put them all in the same box."

Meanwhile I'm tugging at the leg of mom's slacks. "But... can I have a cupcake? Please?"

"No Gordon," she says. "you'll like the raspberry squares."

"What about a lollypop?" I give her my best ever most deserving and plaintive look. It doesn't work. The young woman hands mom a neat brown cardboard box with red string tied around it and mom pays for it. She heads for the door and Vic and I drag our feet.

We're off for White's Stationary Store. Mom wants to get a copy of the local paper and Vic and I are ok with this because they also have a gift shop to ramble around in. Mom knows from experience most of the gift items at White's are also *fragile*, so before complete pandemonium has a chance to break out she gets the paper and hustles us out of there. In a flash, we're off for Hunters.

Grocery stores are boring, so Vic and I opt to stay in the car and eat raspberry squares. "Now leave one for me!" says mom as she scampers into the store. We start munching and we might have left one. Maybe. But probably just one. We don't get into the fig squares. Those are for dad, and because they are known to give the consumer gas, they are best left alone. By the time mom comes out of Hunters, we are well stuffed and the back seat of the car is a flaky crumb mess. After dropping the bags of groceries in the trunk, mom gets in the car sputtering, "The price they want for charcoal briquettes... I just won't pay it! Your father can get some at The First National, until then we'll just have to make do." Vic and I keep quiet and busy ourselves with brushing the crumbs off the seat, onto the plush carpeted floor. Mom then says, "Let's turn on some air…" and Vic and I just look at one another and hunt for our sweaters. We get tangled up in traffic with about fifty other people trying to make the left turn to Wolfeboro Falls at aforementioned traffic-light-free intersection. It takes a half hour to go ¼ mile, but we got *air*. When the smallest gap opens in oncoming traffic mom floors it, avoiding a head-on collision by about two inches, and with a screech of tires and some gnashing of teeth, we're on our way out of the village.

Mr. Moody and his ice house are part of a rapidly dying breed in 1963, and a reminder we can live without things we largely take for granted, like electricity and refrigeration. His home and barn are set on what used to be part of Crescent Lake, but got cut off when the Wolfeboro Railroad built a causeway for the track, forming Goodwin Basin. To step into his barn, a solid timber frame structure right by the water, is to step into a cool and quiet place. Giant mounds of damp sawdust loom in dim light and slight dripping sounds come from unseen places.

Mom and Mr. Moody know one another from way back, so they have things to talk about, like, 'How are the folks?…' They also discuss how big a block of ice mom wants and Mr. Moody, a solid barrel of a man, walks over to one of the mounds and slowly wipes away some sawdust from a spot, and there reveals glistening blocks of ice and the knowledge that deep within there are many, many others. These blocks, and the hundreds more like them he cut from the ice on the lake the previous winter. He wipes a block clean with his hands and grabs it with special tongs and lifts it over his shoulder and onto a leather apron draped across his broad back. He then carries it to the car and sets it in the basin in the trunk. It sits there, sparkling and jewel like with tiny passageways in it from air bubbles that six months ago were trying to get to the surface. The ice is a product of nature, and it's hard to believe it has kept in a pile of sawdust in a barn until this hot summer day.

Mr. Moody's work is quiet, in winter he goes out on the ice with a team of work horses pulling a sledge, and the horses stand and wait while he cuts blocks from the thick frozen surface with special saws. He loads the blocks on the sledge and talking softly to the horses, drives them back to the barn and he tucks the blocks away. Day in and day out, in winter this is what he does. His work has a connection to the rhythms of the seasons and to his horses. There's a certain peace which comes with this. You can see it in Mr. Moody.

We head directly back to the campsite and mom opens the little spigot on the end of the cooler and drains the water from the melted ice onto the ground. It's like the cooler is peeing. For the fun of it Vic and I hold our feet under the stream, and it is some kind of cold! Mom then nestles the new block of ice in the middle of the cooler and arranges the most perishable food close to it. By now it's mid-afternoon, and having survived the heat and commotion of town, it's time for a swim.

. . .

For nearly all of us as we go through life, through adulthood and on to old age the world becomes known, sometimes too well known and dull. For a child exploring the world however, everything is new. Genuinely new. There is brilliance in this, youth is an age of discovery.

It isn't long before Vic and I decide to do some exploring on the water, and Mr. Robie has a couple of well hammered rowboats and a canoe just for this purpose. I'm too young and small to be rowing a boat, but Vic isn't. Mom sets down some limits on where we can go - no further out toward the lake than the marsh, and up Wiley Brook as far as we can get, and if we get to the bridge, there will be no fooling around on the road. For the time being we are to stick with the rowboats. The canoe is just too tippy and I haven't yet figured out how to swim. Mr. Robie fixes us up with oars and floating seat cushions and we're ready for high seas adventure.

The boat is pulled up on shore, and it takes everything we have to push it into the water. Vic gets in first and situates herself on the middle seat facing the stern, and I push us off. Being the navigator I sit up front. We drift while Vic figures out how to get the oars in the locks. The sensation of floating, the subtle fluid motion of drifting and turning is magic, a feeling of no constraints. I watch the water gently eddy and ripple as it passes the bow. A commotion from the engine room snaps me from my daydreaming, I turn to see what's going on with Vic. She's struggling with getting an oar into the lock, it's a hefty thing for a ten year old. She manages to get it in place, the blade is floating in the water, then she turns to set up the other one.

"Vic!" I shout. Her back is to me. She turns and looks at me with some anguish.

"What?" she asks. A sweat is forming on her little brow.

"The oar!" I exclaim, pointing to the oar she got in the lock. It's slowly slipping into the water. She turns to see the last little bit of the handle leave the lock, and it plops into the water. Now the second oar is slipping away like the first.

"Vic!" I again shout and point to the other oar. She looks at me, on the brink of tears. "The other oar!" By now, with the drift of the boat the first oar is beyond arm's reach. She lurches to the other side. The boat is rocking wildly. Vic leans fully over the gunnel and grabs the second oar.

"Help me!" she screams. I jump to her side, it takes the two of us to haul the oar into the boat. With the both of us hanging over the side, the boat tips waaay over. We have the one oar but are steadily drifting away from the first and toward the open lake. A few people gather on the shore.

"Do you need help?" calls a woman.

"We can get it," says Vic. I look at her, wondering how. Vic looks at me and says, "We'll get the oar, don't worry." She starts paddling the boat like a canoe with the one oar, but it begins to turn away from the direction we want to go. Vic hops over to the other side of the boat and putting all her might into it, takes a few strokes. Back and forth she goes and I lean over the bow, ready and stretching to grab the floating oar. Slowly we come up on it and I snatch the handle from the water.

"Got it!" I yell. Vic clamors up beside me and we haul it in. Someone on shore claps. We sit in the boat and look at each other and grin. Lesson #1: do not let go of the oars. "Can we go up the brook?" I ask. We're pointed in this direction, Vic settles in and starts figuring out how to row the boat. Our course is a bit zigzaggy, but we make it past the beach. Some of the kids stand and watch us glide past. "*We* are in a boat, and *you* are stuck on shore," I whisper to Vic and we snicker.

Until you get the hang of it, it's easy to get turned around rowing a boat. First, the rower has their back to the direction of travel. Second, to go right you paddle left. And if your navigator is an excitable kid, well, we easily get turning in the wrong direction, and scrape into rocks and under low hanging branches.

Up front I am the first to break through spider webs, they're all clingy and strange and I don't want to get into trouble with some angry spider. And there are mosquitoes and dense swirling clouds of tiny black gnats. Curious redwing blackbirds cling and wobble on branches and cat-o'-nine-tails and announce our entrance with their screechy whistle. The patch of red on their wings, except for the fluorescent orange painted on the noses of the airplanes dad flies, is the brightest color I've ever seen. We row around a small island. Birds dart and glide from tree to tree, and an occasional fish rises for a bug. Otherwise it is still and quiet in here. When we're in relatively open water, with little chance of running into things, I hang my head over the side and watch the bow wave build and ebb with Vic's rowing. The water is deep and dark, it parts and bubbles and flows to either side of the stem, parting and flowing, endlessly. I drag my fingers in the water and watch the little wakes and eddies.

We come around the island. "I'm getting tired," says Vic. "Let's drift in the current." We can hear kids on the beach around the bend. Noiselessly we drift and every once in a while Vic takes a stroke with an oar to keep us from getting too close to shore. Vic spots a great blue heron in a thicket of grass, taps me on the shoulder and points to it. It stands absolutely still, as though made from stone, but then slowly, on long spindly legs the bird steps forward.

"His knees go backwards," I whisper and giggle. Suddenly, the heron jabs its beak into the water and comes up with a madly wriggling fish, straightens its head in the air and down the hatch goes the fish. It's the biggest bird we've ever seen. We drift close enough to spook it, and in a burst of motion it takes flight, flapping its slate blue wings, its body teeters and tilts and it disappears from view. Vic and I look at one another in awe.

35

More than a few of our camping neighbors are into fishing - it's a big deal for these guys. But most of them are city fellows who love catching fish, but at the end of the day they don't quite know what to do with them. This is where mom comes in. Mom has a saying, "Always make friends with the meat man," and in later years I would see the wisdom in this and use it to good effect at the grocery store. However, given we are now living in the woods near a lake and there are no meat men, let alone grocery stores, the local fishermen are the next best thing. Perhaps they are the better thing. Mr. Robie has a table and chum bucket set up under the pines for cleaning fish, and mom, being a woodswoman at heart knows how to do the job. She makes a deal with a number of the fishermen: she'll clean their catch for a percentage of the finished goods. And so, we always have fresh fish from the lake, pickerel, perch and small mouth bass. She is very handy with her small hunting knife, a gift Auntie Tora brought back for her from Sweden.

As an aside, many years later after mom dies, Vic and I are deciding what to do with what in her house. Antiques and family heirlooms are everywhere, and I open a kitchen drawer and there is the hunting knife. I can see all those times mom standing at that table, cleaning fish. I now have the knife, it means more to me than all the family silver.

When it comes to feeding the ravenous hordes, mom is the boss, but the grill is the man's domain. I've never understood this division of labor, it could be ancient, the building and keeping of fire. The First National back in Concord sells hibachis, little grills which are finished well enough, with golden wood handles and chrome plated grills. Little sliding vents to control heat, sort of. But they are cheap cast pot metal which after a season of grilling will burn to pieces. Nonetheless, the hibachi is dad's deal, and lighter fluid his best friend.

Cooking fillets of fish on a grill takes finesse, something dad has in spades at the controls of an airplane, but sorely lacks in the kitchen. The flesh of a fish is delicate, it cooks in minutes and will stick to the grill in a heartbeat. It does not suffer ham-fisted handling. Dad's grill repertoire includes steaks and burgers and hot dogs. But fillets of fish? No. So mom packages a fillet with a slice of onion and a few chunks of potato in aluminum foil packets and dad puts them on the glowing briquettes. Sometimes we do this on an open camp fire. Full of anticipation we watch tiny geysers of steam erupt from crevices in the packets, we know the combination of flavors are heavenly, especially if the onion burns a bit and caramelizes. You haven't lived until after a day in the open, the fresh air, you've eaten a meal prepared this way, sitting at a picnic table with a view of the lake with people you love, and you know love you. A soft breeze sifts through the pines…

As though the lake will suck us into oblivion, Vic and I are cautious about exploring the marsh. It is a middle place between the safety of the brook and the vastness of open water beyond. But the hummocks of bright green grass brim with life, full of frogs and birds and dragonflies, they call to us. Vic pretty well has the hang of rowing and I'm happy to ride in the bow. One morning we decide to explore the marsh. As we head out the cove opens up. Small waves from the lake lap against the side of the boat. We get closer to the marsh, there's a little inlet which Vic heads for. Bullfrogs, like the rest of us have their comfort zone. When we get a little too close, all of a sudden three or four of them jump from sunning themselves in the grass to the relative safety of the water. Clouds of frog eggs cling to twigs and stalks of grass under water. I reach over the side and grab a handful. They are slimy and cool, each one a translucent globule smaller than a pea with a tiny black dot in the middle.

Vic pivots the oars forward so they're resting in the boat, and comes up to the bow with me. "Those dots are going to be frogs," she says. I look at her, disbelieving and she nods her head. "It's true. Ask mom." Mom is the ultimate authority on everything in nature.

"But frogs are big and green." I say, ever the skeptic.

"You wait. We'll come back and there'll be tadpoles and then pollywogs and then... frogs!" says Vic. "Lots of 'em."

I place the eggs back in the water. The cluster drifts and then sticks to a twig. Redwing blackbirds zoom around catching bugs and screeching. Barb calls them "*skrika*" which is Swedish for scream, and so this is what we call them. *Skrika! Skrika!* Vic noses the boat around, exploring different little places. The water is shallow and warm and the grass is shiny and has sharp edges.

"Do you think it's ok to get out of the boat?" I ask Vic.

"I don't know," she says, hesitant. "Maybe. Go ahead."

"I'm going to try it," I say. I get one leg over the gunnel and dangle my foot in the water. I can't quite touch bottom so I lean further over the side of the boat, pressing my equipment on the gunnel which starts to hurt. So I swing the other leg over and lose my balance and gangly arms and legs go in all directions. I fall in. "Vic!" I yell. When my feet hit the bottom they keep going. It's the most slippery oozy muck, and big bubbles of smelly gas rise from it. I stick a hand out to catch myself, but like my feet when it hits bottom it keeps going. Now I am covered with black muck and flail around. "Vic!" I yell again, but she is in the boat looking at me and laughing her head off.

"You're all mud!" she screams, in hysterics. Having been all stirred up, the water I'm standing in has turned to black soup, and at maybe a foot deep I can't see my feet. We manage to get me back in the boat, I look like a cross between a beached seal and swamp thing, and there's a gritty feeling in my bathing suit that's not too pleasant.

We row around a bit more and see dragonflies, most of them bright blue but some are green or even red and lots more frogs. A breeze comes up from the lake and I'm cold and gritty and not happy and say, "I want to go back."

When we see mom at the campsite we tell her our story and I ask her about frog eggs. She confirms what Vic said and Vic looks smug. When mom sees the mud in my hair, and in my ears and other places she tells me I need to go over to Barb and Pamp's to wash. She hobbles along with me, and even though no one is at the cottage it is wide open. We go inside, the place feels hollow and lonely with Barb and Pamp gone. Mom helps me get the shower going without freezing or scalding myself, and it feels good. The water coming off of me at first is black with mud.

By mid-July it's thunderstorm season. All that heat and lake moisture build and build in the hills, and the wind blows and something has to give. The storms come on suddenly and can be intense. Real snappers. We've run a long extension cord from Barb and Pamp's to the tent, which has been nice. With this we have a small electric table lamp, which is a lot easier to work than the Coleman lantern, and we can listen to the radio. One afternoon the clouds build and we hear soft low rumbling of distant thunder. Suddenly as though someone threw a switch, the sun is gone, all is greyness and a cold wind kicks up off the lake. The surface of the water looks angry, perturbed, black, and whitecaps form on the crests of the waves. From the beach we all scramble for cover. We get to the tent and mom yells, "Zip up the windows, I'll get the door!"

Vic and I run around zipping up windows and not a moment too soon. The wind blows, the tent billows and shifts. It gets dark and mom turns on the table lamp. Tippy squeezes in under the door. He looks at us with wild eyes, like what is going on? Then the rain comes down in buckets, the drumming on the canvas turns to a roar, we stand together in the middle of the tent looking at one another, Tippy is in and out between our legs. Mom is uneasy. Lightning flashes and thunder booms. The time between the flash and the boom is rapidly decreasing until it's Flash! Boom!, and then FLASHBOOM!, then FLABOOM!

The table lamp blows out and with a big spark the cord jumps like a snake. The smell of ozone fills the air and the storm is not letting up. When the lightning flashes it's instantly brighter than daylight and then darkness - FLABOOM! FLABOOM! Sparks fly again and again from the wildly whipping cord. Mom unzips the door, and standing on the now soaking wet canvas floor on her one good leg grabs the cord and throws it outside. Vic and I are standing there agog, jaws dropped.

Ground? Who needs that anyway? Two wires have always gotten the job done... can't see a need for three. This was the end of having an extension cord come out to the tent.

. . .

Vic is four years and 364 days older than me. Our

birthdays are in August, hers one day after mine, and they always get lumped together. The big deal of it is diluted by having to share the celebration, so birthdays are never a completely satisfactory experience. Today, the business of moving holidays around to create long weekends drives me nuts.

It's my sixth birthday, and first thing in the morning I get a card from mom and dad with $6.00 in it. A fortune! That's a lot of money! This evening we will have a party at Barb and Pamp's. I'm all excited and dart in and out of the cottage all day. The smells of the big pan of chili Barb is making and the enchilada casserole with black olives in it are driving me crazy. No bathing suits for this party, late in the afternoon we all get dressed in actual clothes. Except of course shoes. There will be no shoes for at least two more weeks. When we go over to the cottage, I notice neither mom or dad are carrying any presents, and there's no cake and I get nervous. No presents? No cake? But it's my/our birthday. When we get inside the cottage, lo and behold, like magic the picture changes, there's a pile of gifts wrapped in bright paper on the table in the corner. In the kitchen on top of the fridge there's a brown bakery box tied with red string tied around it. It has to be from the Yum Yum Shop. How grown-ups pull things like this off without me knowing about it is impressive. Vic and I are required to be on good behavior, but by now I am so accustomed to being outside, it's a struggle to be indoors long enough to visit and have dinner. With the promise of presents and cake however, I manage. To wait. Patiently. Pretty much.

Barb and Pamp give me a wallet. It's brown plastic stitched with thick white cord around the edges, and on one side is a picture of a cowboy riding a bucking bronco, just like on the Wyoming license plate. His chaps have little panels of fake cowhide complete with bristly hair in patches of brown and white. I open it and find six crisp $1.00 bills in it. I'm rich! I promptly pull the $6.00 mom and dad gave me from my pocket, tuck them in the wallet, fold it and put it in my pocket. I feel like I'm more grown up, men always carry a wallet and it's often a big lump in their back pocket stuffed with all sorts of important things, receipts and photos and even some money. My big present is an HO scale train set, a starter kit with an engine and two cars and a caboose. The track is just a small oval, and we set it up right away on the dining room table. A train set has been on my mind since I saw one, a cool miniature world, set up at French's Toy Store. But with this set, all the train does is go around and around. Ok, the engine has a cool little head lamp that actually works. Even though I give it my best effort for the next six months, I'm bored with it. It will turn out I'm much more interested in slot cars because I can race my friends and dad, even though dad almost always wins.

When we get back to the tent it's dark and dad lights the Coleman lantern. It floods the interior with bright white light. The weather in August in New Hampshire signals the end of summer and the lantern takes the chill off the air. Swamp maples are already turning red. I get in my sleeping bag and lay there for a while, looking at the cowboy on my wallet and quickly fall off to sleep.

Although the reasons I now live in the west are many, these two cowboys planted "head west young man," in my imagination. And whatever fills our imagination is the starting place of adventure… and for me, the further flung, the better.

. . .

Mr. Robie and Pamp were young men during the Great Depression and like many others, they can build something out of practically nothing. What they accomplish is always cobbled together, but it usually works. It's an admirable way of doing things, recognizing, 'we may not have much, but we're going to do this anyway and it's going to be an improvement.' By golly. When we return the next summer, the outhouse is gone and like magic a genuine bath house stands in its place, with septic system no less, and is ready for customers.

It's an imposing edifice, a solid grey cement block structure with a pitched roof. The cement walls are unfinished and inside there is no ceiling. Calling it a cathedral ceiling is far too high and mighty. This after all ain't no cathedral. The roof is translucent green fiberglass panels, which provide illumination during the day. Inside, everyone looks either seasick or about ready to die, but marginally better at night when the one bare light bulb hanging in the center of the building comes on. In the men's side there is a sink with cold water spigot only and a mirror, two toilets in rickety plywood stalls and a separate small private space for changing and a shower. Water is drawn from the lake, and in the corner is a pump and pressure tank and a hot water heater. Pipes to the various fixtures run in all zigzag directions overhead. The temperature of the shower is not adjustable. Somewhere in the works is a thingamabob which blends hot and cold, and there's just one valve at the shower head.

Using the shower for the first time, even though I am now well into being six with my own cowboy wallet and everything, requires great bravery. This is not like at home, and I'm on my own. With the door latched I put my towel and soap on the bench in the changing area and then take my clothes off - except for the flip-flops mom insists we wear so we don't get athlete's foot, which we get anyway. To turn on the water I have to stand in my tender nakedness where it will start spraying. Surrounded by cement I'm already cold, nonetheless I stand there, turn on the valve and the first squirt of water is like ice cubes. The trick is to leap out of the way without slipping and falling, which would not be good. The floor is less than tidy and I don't want athlete's body - in a manner of speaking. The water warms up in a moment and I get under the spray. You get what you get, and when the hot water heater runs out, which happens in about three minutes, what you get is cold. This must be by design. Mr. Robie doesn't want to be paying a hot water bill for dilly-dallying in this shower, no-sah.

There are vents in the peaks of the roof but no fans. Bug control consists of curlicue strips of flypaper hanging down, which don't get changed very often so they are covered with dead and struggling flies and are disgusting. Even though it's cold and clammy and smelly and green and gross in the bath house, it's still a thousand percent improvement over the outhouse. Still, nothing beats bathing in the lake in the dark, but even in the early 1960's we know that's just not "environmentally friendly," in quotes because no one has actually thought to put these two words together yet.

Mr. Robie is a friendly guy and rides around on his Ford tractor and loves to stop and talk. Why he goes around on the tractor is not readily apparent - he must simply like driving it because he's certainly not doing any tractor work with the thing. He comes chugging by and if he sees one of us he'll wave, and we wave back and this is taken as an invitation for him to stop. Of course we always wave because it's polite and he's a friendly guy so this means he always stops. He leaves the tractor running and he can't hear very well, so he hops down and talks and talks and talks. Thick black smoke puffs past the flipper on the end of the exhaust stack. My calculations indicate the gallons of diesel he burns this way over the years could power the U.S. Naval fleet for a week. Mr. Robie is soft spoken and when he gets going, totters back and forth from foot to foot. If the topic of conversation gets him excited, such as anything remotely liberal he totters faster.

I'm just about to go hunt some frogs and here comes Mr. Robie on the tractor and he waves. I want to pretend I don't see him but it's too late, he saw me looking at him, so I wave back. He stops and sets the brake which makes a heavy metallic ratcheting sound, and once satisfied the tractor isn't going to roll away he hops down.

"Morning Mr. Robie," I say.

"Mawnin Gawdin." he says. He has a twinkle in his eye. "What chu gonna do with that bucket?" he queries.

"I'm going to catch some frogs," I say.

"Ehya, ehya, ehya…" says Mr. Robie. Whenever someone else is talking he says this just above a whisper, in a sing-song way. Each "ehya" the product of a short inhale or exhale.

"What's that, Mr. Robie?" I ask. He looks at me, puzzled. I fidget because I'd like to get going. Mr. Robie totters because that's what he does.

"What chu gonna do with'm once you catch'm?" he asks.

I shrug my shoulders. "I dunno," I say.

"Well, please be shuah put'm back in tha watah when yew through with'm. They's livin things, an they eat lotsa bugs, you know," he says. "Plus, I love hear'n'em croakin' into the night."

"Yes, Sir," I say. "I will."

"Thank you," he says, and goes on, "Ah your mutha or fatha heah?"

"No Sir. Mom's at the beach and dad's in Concord," I say.

"Whuts he doin in Cawncud?" he asks. That's the state capitol. Now he's tottering faster.

"Dad's at work," I say.

"Oh. Well Ima goin around lettin' folks know tonight's the night Im gonna staht usin muy new bug foggah. Just soz you know," he says. "Ain't like the place is catchin on fiah or nothin!" He laughs, takes off his cap and pushes back the shock of white hair atop his head. He's got a shave on the sides and long hair on top. Then he methodically puts his cap back on.

I've never heard of anything like this before. "Mr. Robie, what's a 'bug foggah'?" I ask.

"Well Gawdin, yull see. It'sa new device Im tryin. Makes smoke and kills them skeetahs," he says. "I'll be goin round with it just at sunset tonight. First tyme withit."

"O.K. Mr. Robie. I'll let mom and dad know," I say. I really want to be catching some frogs.

"Thank you Gawdin. Watch out fah pickerel when yew out theyah," says Mr. Robie. I wonder what's a 'pickrel' but I don't ask. Mr. Robie gets on the tractor, releases the brake and chugs over to the next campsite. I see him wave to someone, he's got 'em.

In time I learn if Mr. Robie is cleaning the bath house and some hapless soul, like me, should come along needing, say, to use the toilet, he will intercept them to have a talk, completely oblivious to the fact this person has their legs crossed and is breaking out in a sweat. The strategy is, if I see him anywhere near the bath house, to wait if I can until he is gone or he's caught someone else giving me the opportunity to slip by.

I go out to the marsh. The sun is intense. The skin on my back, what's left of it, immediately gives me the warning signal a burn is eminent. I choose to ignore it. It's so hot not even the *Skrika's* are out. There are dragonflies, their wings make a faint ticking sound as they zoom by. I pad through the weeds, keeping very quiet. The edges of the grass cut against my legs and the pointy ends of the blades are sharp. The serious frog hunter must be stealthy and persevere even in the most adverse conditions. I move slow and quiet, and spot my prey. A giant old croaker right on the edge of a grass hummock. The frog sits perfectly still, deep in his frog thoughts, I don't think he sees me. I just know he's headed for my bucket. Inching my way toward him, I begin to outstretch my arm, and... *boing!* He leaps into the water, takes a few strokes with his powerful hind legs and is gone. This happens a few more times. I'm burned to a crisp and my legs are cut up and I'm thirsty and my bucket is frog-less. Time to regroup, go back to home base and have a Kool-Aid. And maybe a raspberry square if there are any left.

Mom's at the tent when I get back. "How was frog hunting?" she asks.

"I saw lots of them but I didn't get any," I say. "They're quick." I pour myself a glass of bright red Kool-Aid. "Can I have a raspberry square?" I ask.

"No, Dear, it's almost time for lunch," says mom.

"Aw, c'mon..." I plead.

"No. Let's make some tuna salad," she suggests. "Were you in the grass or in the water, hunting frogs?" she asks.

I look at my mom. "In the grass," I say.

"Try wading in the water. This way, when they get scared they'll jump toward you," she says.

I am astonished. "How did you know that?" I ask.

Mom looks up from digging around for a can of tuna, she looks at me and smiles. "I've caught a frog or two," she says. "Would you get the celery out of the cooler, please?" It's amazing how smart grown-ups can be.

After lunch I have a raspberry square. The last one, ha ha! Wait 'til Vic finds out. "I'm going frog hunting again." I say.

"I think you've had enough sun," says mom. "How about staying around here for a while?"

"Oh, O.K.," I say. "Want to play pick-up-sticks?" I ask.

"Sure," says mom.

I get the tube filled with the thin bright colored plastic sticks. "Where do you want to play?" I ask.

"How about the foot of your sleeping bag?" she suggests.

"O.K.," I say, and head over to my cot. I love walking barefoot on the tent's canvas floor, it's cool and dry. You can feel how rugged the fabric is and at the same time feel the irregularities of the ground beneath it. I toss the pile of sticks on my sleeping bag and the game has begun. It's so exciting, at some point mid-game I fall asleep and nap. I think this was mom's idea all along. Just writing about pick-up-sticks makes me sleepy.

It's mid-afternoon when I wake up, and we all go to the beach for a swim. Well, mom and Vic go for a swim. I flail around. Because Vic and I are making frequent use of the rowboats, and we have our eyes on the canoe, and we also have our eyes on the lake, mom has decided it's time for me to learn how to swim. Oh, silly mom. This is just the beginning of finding out just how uncoordinated I am. Fortunately she starts me out with the dog paddle, but there's this thing called "the crawl," she's talking about. Mom and Vic both do the crawl. So, mom gets in the water with me and holds me under my belly and describes how to keep my head above water and paddle my arms and legs. I'm nervous and thrash around. "No… not like that," she says. "Here, watch me do it." And mom dog paddles.

There are other kids in the water and a couple of them have big white Styrofoam capsules strapped to their backs, so they float. "Why can't I have one of those?" I ask.

"If you get used to having one, you'll never learn how to swim," says mom. "And then, if you fall out of a boat what are you going to do?"

I never do like it when what grown-ups say is contrary to my way of thinking yet makes perfect sense. "O.K.…," I say. So we try the dog paddle over and over and over again. When I start to get it, mom drops her arms away from underneath me, and I stop and stand there.

She looks at me and grins. "Now Gordon. You're doing the dog paddle. You can do it on your own. Now let's try again," she says. And we do, and eventually, she drops her arms away and I just keep going. "You're swimming!" she yells triumphantly, as I'm chugging away.

I stop and stand up. "What?" I ask.

She shakes her head. "I said, you're swimming. I'm very proud of you. Now try it again on your own," she says, and I do. I become a very proficient dog paddler.

When dad gets home - the lake is not official home home, but it's home - we have supper and I mention Mr. Robie is going to be using a "bug foggah" tonight. Mom corrects me. "It's a bug fogger," she says, adding, "It's not polite to imitate Mr. Robie."

"Why not?" I ask. "He talks funny, and imitating him is fun."

"This may be true, but it's just the way he learned to talk. It's called an accent," says mom. "Like your cousins from Texas. They have an accent that's different from Mr. Robie's. We all have accents, we do too, but because we're used to it we don't think about it," she says. "But it's not polite to imitate, so please don't do it."

"O.K.," I say. But this isn't any fun.

There's a pungent, acrid chemical smell in the air. We look around the side of the tent and here comes Mr. Robie, waving around this hissing, smoking contraption. "Speak of the Devil," says dad. "Here comes Mr. Robie with the bug foggah." He grins.

"Bunk!" Mom admonishes him. "You're not being any help!"

Before we know it, the entire campground is enveloped in a thick oily cloud. The stuff stinks bad. Vic and I pull up our t-shirts over our faces.

"I can see your belly button!" I say, muffled, pointing at Vic, and I laugh. She struggles with what to do. Keep her t-shirt up over her face or cover her belly button.

"Well, smarty-pants. I can see yours!" she says. And now the joke's on me. I'm a pudgy little kid and sure enough, my roll of a belly is sticking out and there's my belly button, a little deeper than it should be. I decide it'll be fun to chase Vic around. I leap at her and she lunges away and off we go into the cloud.

"You two!" yells mom. "Be careful!"

The smoke is awful. We see Mr. Robie coming around the bend, so we head full tilt for the lake where there's enough of a breeze so the air is clear. Amazing, that somehow our entire generation didn't all produce offspring with three arms and flippers. But when Mr. Robie went around with his foggah, you bettah believe, thar warnt no skeetahs aftah that. No-sah!

There are other, less toxic but no more tasteful counter-bug-terror measures taken at the campground. Hanging in a tree outside the men's side of the bath house, and I wonder why it's the men's and not the lady's side - Mr. Robie apparently has a sense of chivalry or maybe it is just closest to the only electrical outlet - is a fluorescent bug sucker. This device consists of a blue color circular ring fluorescent lamp hanging vertically with a fan behind it. The air the fan sucks in is blown into a plastic bag below. Night falls and you're a hapless bug flying around looking for someone's blood to suck, or maybe a mate, and there's that light. Will ya look at that light. And you're drawn to it, you can't help yourself, so you fly over in that direction and it looks even better. You see some of your pals heading over too. So you zoom in for an even closer look, and there's a breeze, and the breeze turns into a wind, and sss-whaaa-*suck!* You get pulled into the vortex of rushing air and whammo! Now you're trapped in a plastic bag with a bazillion other bugs, most dead, many mortally wounded calling for a medic, some buzzing around and going manic and now you're part of the bunch, all with a certain, grim end.

After a busy night of bug sucking, the bag is packed full and writhing. This is something we men, reluctantly, have to face when we make our morning trip to the bath house.

In addition to the suckers, there are the bug zappers. Mr. Robie has a few of these hanging in trees around the place, but the best one is in town outside Bailey's Ice Cream.

Because we have only a cooler, which is not capable of keeping ice cream frozen, getting an ice cream means a trip into town, usually at night. Going into Wolfeboro at night is special. There are boys and girls running around, it's where the action is. When you're six, it doesn't take much to be exciting. By the time you're ten however, Wolfeboro is dullsville. Then, by sixteen it's interesting again. Girls, you know. But I digress. Bailey's is as much a road side institution as it is restaurant, and they have an ice cream counter in front. The place is all lit up with fluorescent tubes under the eaves, and there's lots of happy people milling around, happy because everyone is either anticipating or eating the most delicious ice cream in the world. So with all the bright light, and the concentration of warm blooded bodies in the same place, there are also many, many bugs. Millions of them. Mosquitoes mostly, and if you have a magnifying glass handy you'd see they're all smiling too. Ice cream, humans and blood. Let's party!

So the nice folks at Bailey's hang a bug zapper right above the crowd. People are standing there eating their ice creams and a constant flow of bugs, drawn from the whole Lakes Region, are wondering, "eenie meenie miney mo… warm body or blue light?", and the ones who go for the light… before they get to it… ZZAP! They are gonzo. Natural selection at work.

Now *my* family being a collective of smarty-pants thinks this is pretty funny, and we watch people standing under the bug zapper going, ZZAP!… ZZAP!… and ZZZZAP! (The extended zap is for a June bug.) And what those people under the thing apparently are not realizing is the well toasted remains of bugs are falling from the zapper onto them and the ice creams they're madly licking at. Ha Ha! We imagine people being puzzled. "Hey, I didn't order chocolate sprinkles on my double dip peppermint stick…"

. . .

When we're kids, grown-ups are mysterious, just plain strange, and it's usually not until we grow up ourselves we realize it's life itself that makes us this way. By the time it's happening to us, we like to call it "complex."

Dad is a quiet guy. Vic and I, not to his face, at different times refer to him as "The Classic Clam." What is going on in there is a great unknown. But for dad like all of us, it's life. Being eight years old right after the depression and having his father die, then as a young guy flying bombers in three wars and getting shot at a bunch of times, then as it all wears on, liberally apply three or four scotches every night to keep all this stuff back in a corner somewhere, well… this isn't exactly the path to being open. But bless his heart, he still finds ways of showing his love.

Every once in a while in the evening, we have a visit from Mickey Mouse, or rather, dad's Mickey Mouse hand puppet.

The puppet is a relic from dad's childhood, the body made of black velvet with stuffed hands and head. Mickey's hands and face are yellow-ish fabric, and even though he's very well worn his eyes are still bright. In Walt Disney's cartoons, Mickey is known as an ever cheerful and shy little character, which dad carries on to his puppet's antics. Mickey never makes a sound.

We're hanging around the tent. "Look! There's Mickey!" squeals Vic. I turn my head around quick as I can and catch a glimpse of a mouse peeking over the edge of the table. And pop! He disappears.

"Where's Mickey?" we ask. And we wait. And wait. And when we just about can't stand it anymore... pop! Mickey appears from behind the Coleman lantern. This time he looks at us. We say, "Hi Mickey!" maybe a little too loud for him. He retreats, but is still peeking at us. And if we're quiet for a moment he edges out and with one little hand, shyly waves. Vic and I are filled to the brim with joy. And if we're still, Mickey, ever so slowly crawls toward us... we have to sit still... and he disappears under the cot we're sitting on. Suddenly, Vic's face lights up, she is about to burst. She can feel Mickey crawling up her back. I lean around and can see him. He stops and looks at me and holds his hand up to his mouth. "Shhh..." Oh, he's trying to surprise Vic, who is by now a complete squirm-ball. Mickey slowly makes his way up Vic's back. She turns her head looking for him over her shoulder but he isn't there... yet. We two sit very, very still. And Vic feels Mickey advancing, and pop! He appears over Vic's shoulder. She jumps, Mickey retreats and then appears again and waves to me and motions a hand for me to come closer. And I lift my hand toward him and he extends his. He looks at Vic, tilting his head as if to ask, "think this is ok?" Vic nods. Mickey and I shake hands. Mickey then looks at Vic and nods and then he reaches up and pats Vic on the cheek. Vic melts, turns and kisses him. Bashful, he turns away and covers his face with his hands. Slowly he then draws his hands away and looks at Vic, rapt. He then places his hands over his heart...

Sometimes Mickey shows up around the campfire, especially when other kids are around. Every face around the fire, young and old, is filled with joy. These moments are some of the happiest in our lives.

.   .   .

On the other end of the spectrum, there's laundry. Sooner or later the mounting odorous pile needs to be faced. This means a trip to Auntie Tora's and a lot of rather boring hanging out, but it also means we'll go by Gene's and if we're good, this means we'll get an ice cream out of the deal. Of course mom is clever. We pass Gene's on the way to Auntie's and we're begging for ice cream. "When we come back," she says, adding, "We don't want to spoil our lunch at Auntie's." She must not realize Vic and I are more than happy to spoil our lunch. Auntie is generous to cook a lunch for us, but there are only so many boiled dinners a kid can ingest in a lifetime. Anyway, mom's strategy is to hold the ice creams over our heads as bait for good behavior until *after* we've spent the day at Auntie's, and it usually works to good effect.

We live for the most part in bathing suits, so laundry consists of bathing suits, lots of sandy beach towels, a few pillow cases, that's about it. Still, it adds up to a few loads, and going to Auntie's sure beats the hours in the Laundromat in Wolfeboro Falls. That place is always jammed, it's 105 degrees in there, and has to be a total cash machine. We stuff our dirties in the pillow cases and we're off. The Lake Road, as we call it, is all twists and turns along the shore, we go past Wentworth State Park which is always crawling with people, and the smells of fifty cookouts floods the air. We are hungry. Vic and I are always hungry. And then it's the public beach which is equally crowded and Gene's is right across the road. I look at the place longingly as we fly past.

There are a number of small camps along the road at this end of the lake. It's low and marshy land, and between black flies and mosquitoes, I guess this explains why we never see anyone outside. One of the camps has a split rail fence out front and perched on top of each post is a clear liquor bottle, each filled with colored water. They're all different and brilliant. "Why no one's shot at them, I don't know," mom wonders aloud. Her wondering suggests she's thought about shooting them. Another of mom's woodswoman skills happens to be she's an excellent shot. I love to look at them, all bright and colorful and twinkly. Where we turn onto Bryant Road, there's a tall sign listing the names of all the folks living in the area. Including "V. Nelson," that's Auntie, and, "A. Nelson" her brother Arvid, a.k.a. Pamp. Barb and Pamp haven't lived in Cotton Valley for years. A lot of the people whose names appear on that sign haven't lived here for a long time. If I were to go to the turnoff today, I wouldn't be surprised to see the sign unchanged, even though at this point most of those old folks are dead. Frankly I'd be flabbergasted if anything has changed. It's quiet in Cotton Valley.

At Frost Corner we turn on to Cotton Valley Road. This is where the road turns to dirt and it is one whoop and dip after another. I love the feeling of the big Buick going airborne, well, almost airborne over the whoops. Mom toodles right along. Dad calls her "Old Lead Foot," a nickname she takes a certain pleasure in. A few times every summer the road crew comes along and sprays the road with waste oil to keep the dust down (again, the EPA hasn't been invented yet). Imagine dumping hundreds of gallons of toxic oil on the ground. Ground? Ground water? "Ehya, we know 'bout ground watah. S'down theyah somwheyah. Ain't nawthin t'worry 'bout."

Auntie's house is the cutest little white clapboarded Cape by the side of the road, with an ancient stone wall of neatly stacked granite boulders pulled when fields got cleared, now all covered with lichen. There's a big maple tree out front and pines in the back. Around the house are lilacs and viburnum, and in the back yard Auntie grows tall, flashy gladiolas. Auntie Tora is cool. She was a kid when her family immigrated to the United States from Sweden. Photos of her as a young woman reveal she was a hottie, and there was never a shortage of boyfriends. In a small town, a good looking single woman... there was also never a shortage of stories. Auntie traveled on her own, by freighter to Sweden, across North America by train or car, sometimes meandering through the Southwest, and often to visit a cousin in Vancouver, British Columbia. She owned two of the first Saab cars to come to the U.S. and crossed the country in them. She used a fountain pen filled with "Peacock Blue" ink to write postcards from all those exotic places in the most beautiful flowing script handwriting you'll ever see.

Today, life is less glamorous. Despite the windows being open, the little house stinks like boiling cabbage and turnip. Auntie loves to see us, but at the same time she's always a little apprehensive. Her house, and all her furnishings and decorations are just so, and Vic and I are a couple of little redheaded wild things. We haven't lived with solid walls for nearly two months, nor have we even put on shoes. Mom reminds us of an ice cream at Gene's which has somewhat of a calming effect, so she's confident it's O.K. to go into the basement and start a load of laundry. No way will I go down there. Auntie's cellar is a scary place, with a narrow, steep stairway, and cobwebs and exposed stones in the foundation and one bare bulb to light it all. Just peeking down the stairs is enough for me, and imagine, if you are down there and the bulb blows out! All manner of goblins and ghosts would come out of the cracks. Fortunately mom never asks me to come help with the laundry. She probably finds some relief in those few spare moments of solitude down there.

Auntie has a thing for African Violets. They're in every window, cushions of fuzzy little leaves and diminutive blossoms of pink and lavender and white. Her showpiece is a plant with deep violet double blossoms in a special pot in the window over the kitchen sink. The pot is ceramic with frogs holding hands as if caught in a dance around the circumference of it. Also in her kitchen is a collection of colorful Italian blown glass animals on the sills of the south facing windows. I'm fascinated with them, the fanciful roosters and tigers glitter and twinkle in the sun. Her little house is a magical place. She had it built in the 1940's, only after working on the local banker's unwillingness to make her a loan. It had nothing to do with her ability to pay it back; it was a whole new thing to him, loaning money to a woman, much less a single one...

"Why, we've never heard of such a thing Tora," blusters the banker.

"You have now," says Auntie, not easily put off. It takes a while, but she wears him down. And I wouldn't put it past her if she flirted with him, a tiny little bit, to get the old geezer all excited and on her side. She lived in the little house on Cotton Mountain Road called "Anatora" for over fifty years.

The laundry grinds away in the basement and Vic and I take turns having a bath. This is a big treat, a whole tub full of hot water and no cold cement walls. There's the National Geographic map wallpaper and the room smells like flowers and talcum powder. Looking at maps is so much fun, all the far away places with funny names, mountains and rivers, and soaking in hot water is a recipe for daydreaming and letting the imagination roam… and sometimes nodding off…

There I am, on safari, surrounded by bare-breasted women deep in the brush of Tanzania. Wow this is great, until… there's a knock on the door. "Gordon? You haven't drowned in there?" mom asks.

"Uh… no I'm…" I say. Darn. We'd just got a report from the scout he'd seen the elusive albino Rhino we'd been tracking all day, right outside camp. The women, fearful of Rhino attack, scatter. I hate it when this happens.

"Dinner's ready," says mom. "Don't dilly-dally."

I'll be out in a minute," I say. I get up out of the tub and step onto the poofy mat on the floor, grab a towel and dry myself off - except I'm sweating from lounging in a tub of hot water. And to top it off, I now have to face a steaming boiled dinner on this equally steaming July afternoon. I weigh in my mind just how important an ice cream at Gene's is anyway.

After pulling on a pair of shorts and a t-shirt I make my appearance. The dining room table is set, and there's a lot of commotion in the kitchen. Mom's helping Auntie but what she doesn't get is that in this house, Auntie is the boss, not her. So there's always a spat on the horizon, and all non-essential personnel stay clear of the kitchen. I go into the living room, being careful how I step on the floor. If you're barefoot, like I am, and you step on a seam between the hardwood boards, they come together and pinch your foot. The boards are narrow which makes it tricky. Dad's sitting in the Lincoln rocker looking at a copy of *The Granite State News*. He looks at me and smiles and raises his eyebrows, confirming he and I are together and staying away from the kitchen. Vic is sitting on the sofa looking at a picture book on Andrew Wyeth. Looking at "Christina's World" is a lot like eating boiled dinners.

Mom and Auntie manage to avoid an all out cat fight (this time) and Auntie calls, "Dinner's ready!" Her voice, just a touch shrill. We get up and amble into the dining room. Towers of steam rise from big platters and serving dishes, and Auntie chirps, "Now sit down and eat before it gets cold!"

"O.K. Auntie," we say. "Thank you Auntie. It all looks lovely..." And of course it is, but we're all wishing it was December. In the backs of our minds we know we'll get our wish, when we come to Auntie's just before Christmas for the candle light service at the Cotton Mountain Church. And we'll have a boiled dinner.

A big hot plate of food gets set before me. Being subject to rampant cell division I am always starving so I'm happy to eat. A lot. But heat radiates from the plate and I feel my face flush, rivulets of sweat pour from my armpits. The undersides of my thighs stick to the chair cushion. Auntie fans herself with her napkin. "I must be having a hot flash," she titters.

I want to say, "No Auntie, it's just 118 degrees in here. You're ok." But I manage to keep my mouth shut. Everyone's beginning to get the idea I'm a smarty-pants anyway, so there's no need to flat out confirm this and blow my chances of an ice cream later, which right about now is looking really good.

We make it through dinner and Auntie says, "I have a dessert! Nothing fancy."

"What is it Auntie?" asks Vic. I sit there and hope and pray it's not a peach cobbler fresh out of the oven.

"Something nice and cool," she says. "Jell-O with fruit cocktail in it, with whipped cream." She beams. A sigh of relief goes around the table.

Last winter I was sick and to make a long story bearable, all I ate for a month was Jell-O and broth. Seriously. Doctor's orders. Yes, the way I came out of that one I made a toothpick look fat, and even today, I steer clear of Jell-O. And broth. But in this case the redeeming factors are coolness and the fruit cocktail. Despite it being a flavorless collection of fruit chunks in a sugar syrup from a can, the half slices of vaguely red bing cherries are the prizes. Vic and I, charming little children that we are call them bloody frog's eyes. And the whip cream doesn't hurt.

Auntie and mom and Vic clear the table and dad and I retreat to the living room. Dad goes back to the paper, and I study the *Old Farmer's Almanac*. August is supposed to be rainy and it's going to be a colorful fall. There are instructions on how to do useful things like splice rope and hypnotize lobsters. Vic meanders into the living room with us. She's smart. She knows what's coming.

We can hear Auntie and mom clattering around in the kitchen. It's close quarters in there. "Elna, dear, would you get the cream from the ice box for me?" asks Auntie.

The refrigerator door opens, there's some shuffling around. Mom must have the cream. "Here it is... would you like me to whip it for you?" asks mom.

"No thank you, dear," says Auntie.

"I'd be happy to," says mom. "Here, let me do that for you."

"No dear, I can do this myself," says Auntie with a slight yet distinct edge of irritation rising in her voice.

"It will only take me a minute," says mom.

"No Elna, I'll whip the cream," says Auntie. "Why don't you serve the Jell-O?"

Mom says nothing. There's some clattering. We can hear Auntie hand cranking her ancient beater like a mad woman.

"You don't have an *electric* mixer?" asks mom. This, being a rhetorical question, is the real beginning of a cat fight.

"No Elna," says Auntie, more than edgy. "You know I do not have an electric mixer."

"Well. I've never understood why," says mom.

"Dear," says Auntie, exasperated and losing her breath from cranking the hand mixer. "I don't want one. I don't *like* electric mixers." She cranks the beater faster and faster.

"An electric mixer would be so much easier," says mom. "It's time to get with it Auntie, get with the 20th Century!" There's a pause. "Careful," says mom, "you don't want to end up with a bowl of butter."

There is silence. We in the living room hold our breaths. Auntie stops whipping the cream and we can hear her *whack! whack! whack!*, rapping the mixer on the side of the bowl. "Dear," says Auntie, her voice is stern, "would you kindly put whip cream on the servings of Jell-O?" She gets no response. And with this Auntie comes into the living room, wiping her hands on her apron, her face is flushed and she's looking like she's about to explode. "Dessert," she sighs, "is ready."

We gather in the dining room and sit down. Tension settles in the air, thick and heavy as the whipped cream, as we quietly start on our desserts.

"The dessert, everything Tora, has been delightful, thank you," says dad.

"Thanks for dessert, Auntie," says Vic.

"You're welcome my dear," says Auntie.

"Well. I know what you're getting for Christmas!" says mom to Auntie, all perky like.

Auntie glares at mom. If she was a cat, she'd have her ears laid back. Her chest heaves and she sighs. "I hope it will be a nice surprise," she says. I have no idea what mom got Auntie for Christmas that year, but if it was an electric mixer, I'll bet you the last cookie it never came out of the box and went straight to the hospital fair. As an aside, when Cool Whip gets invented, it comes as no surprise Auntie immediately changes over to it and never looks back.

We're finished with dessert and it's time to go. "Would you like some help with the dishes?" asks mom.

"No." says Auntie. She's now got her feet planted. "Thank you dear, I'll take care of it." When mom starts carrying a couple dishes into the kitchen Auntie blocks her way. "Here, I'll take those." The party is over and she wants us out. Mom at least.

"Let's all change into our suits before we go," says mom. "We'll stop for a swim at the public beach on the way back to Robie's."

We all think this is a wonderful idea, especially Vic and me because we know this is code for "we'll go to Gene's for an ice cream." With our suits on, and two big baskets of damp laundry (Auntie has no dryer), we say our thank yous and good byes and we pile into the Buick and head for the beach.

The public beach faces winds from the west and a long stretch of open water. Big waves build and come crashing in, which is quite different from the protected cove at Robie's. One after the other the waves slap on the beach, usually carrying bits and pieces of pine needles and cones and fresh water clam shells. Because of the waves, the sand here is free of slime and muck, and the beach is a long gentle slope into the crystal clear water. In short, this is a great place to swim.

Of course Vic and I are eager to cash in on our good behavior, so we are in favor of going to Gene's first. This requires crossing the road, which is busy, and even though it's late afternoon the black pavement is sizzling hot on our bare feet. So Vic and I each take one of mom's hands, we all look both ways and when the coast is clear we run. Well, Vic and I run and sort of drag mom with us.

Gene's is in a dilapidated, low slung shack with big screened windows all across the front, and decorated with brightly painted pressed metal signs that look like giant ice cream cones, Eskimo pies and other confections. They are a promise of the refreshing sweet treats within, and the promise is never broken. Inside it's dim and cool, and picnic tables are lined up next to the windows. Beckoning pinball machines blink and clang in the back. Along the side, various humming coolers are lined up near the counter. Displays of candy fill every nook and cranny. Essentially it is sugar rush heaven. Gene is there, soft spoken, with twinkly eyes, a broad smile and a brush cut hair cut. He's one of the friendliest guys on earth. We investigate the inventory. The ice cream coolers have sliding glass tops and blow hot air on your feet. The drink cooler is a lot like ours back at the tent, but painted red with "Enjoy Coca Cola" stenciled on it. This one Gene fills with drinks and ice in the morning. By this time of day, most of the ice is melted and you have to fish for the bottles in water that's so cold your hands hurt in no time. But we're interested in ice cream and we have to study them all before making our selections. I get a Creamsicle (still one of my favorites), and Vic gets an Klondike Eskimo Pie with a polar bear on the wrapper. I hear these things are now called "Inuit pies" because Eskimo is no longer culturally acceptable. It appears we're making some progress.

Mom and Gene chitchat for a few minutes while Vic and I busy ourselves with out treats. Once you take the thing from the cooler, the race is on, to inhale it before it melts and runs down your arm or falls apart. Mom and Gene are barely past hello and we are finished and ready to go. Our hands are sticky messes. "You two, don't touch anything with those hands," says mom, and then to Gene, "looks like we need to go for a swim." Gene smiles and thanks us. "Wait for me to cross the road with you," says mom in the voice of authority. We know this voice means business and we do not mess with it. So she opens the screen door with the spring on it that goes "SPROING!" and we exit. "Remember, wait for me," she says and we do. We get to the edge of the pavement and she takes our hands. This has to be gross, maybe not as gross as some motherly duties, but still. We wait for the coast to clear and go for it, and she doesn't let go of us until we're at the water. "Let's wash our hands," she says. With those cool clear waves before us, Vic and I opt for jumping in..

There's no rope, no life guard, no nothing here except beach and you're on your own. Vic and I are having a first rate splash fight and dad takes his shirt off, gosh he's a big and hairy thing. Mom takes off her hat and all of a sudden she looks five sizes smaller. She is famous for big floppy hats in the summer, preferably with a garish peony-like artificial flower attached. Mom loves to swim, for miles if she has the opportunity. Dad can take it or leave it. Vic is a good swimmer and I'm still flailing around. So mom takes off, Vic swims nearby and dad and I stay where I can touch bottom and pretend we're motorboats.

. . .

The rain can pour down briefly with a passing thunderstorm, or it can rain for days, subsiding only now and then to a drizzle. We've learned our lesson about extension cords, and how to handle the wind and crashing and banging of thunderstorms, and we're also learning how to manage a week of wet and grey and cold.

When a thunderstorm approaches we rush around and gather up whatever might blow away, batten down the hatches and hold tight. Tippy comes running inside, squeezing through the unzipped bottom of the door. If he's wet he shakes himself and looks at us and meows and one of us will grab a towel and rub him dry. Even though he gets fidgety, he purrs and purrs. If lightning and thunder are snapping around he crawls into a sleeping bag and hides. We sit in the tent and look at each other and watch the walls rock and sway in the wind, and hope the tent doesn't collapse. The rain, and sometimes hail, roar on the canvas, and we hope none of the big old pines we're nestled beneath is going to come crashing down on top of us. If the rain comes down hard for a while, little streams of water eventually find their way inside and trickle across the floor. They're fun to watch, and wonder which way they'll go. It's all great wildness, being out there in severe weather.

We emerge from the tent after such a storm, and the air, the world, is rinsed clean. Everything is fresh, it is calm, and the lake is like glass. Water drips from the trees, the big drops spatter on the ground. I listen to them, reporting in from here and there. Big puddles stand in the low places, full of floating pine needles, they're fun to walk in, unable to see the bottom, each step a sudden mystery solved.

When wet weather settles in, it's usually dad's job, as he's the tallest, to clip giant sheets of clear plastic around the perimeter of the front awning with as many clothes pins as he can get his hands on, and weigh the bottom down with pieces of firewood and stones. This creates another room - after a day or two with four of us cooped up in the tent we can use all the room we can get. Mom brings in the collection of games and jigsaw puzzles from the trunk of the Buick. Parcheesi, Chinese checkers, Yahtzee, decks of sticky cards, the Ouija board, pickup sticks, tiddlywinks, and Scrabble. We set up a folding card table in the middle of the main room and sit on lawn chairs. The Coleman lantern hisses and floods the place with light and takes the chill off. Rain patters above, there is no sound as soothing as rain falling on a tent. We have insulated plastic mugs we got as free gifts for spending money at the First National, and drink hot tea and hot chocolate from them. Hot chocolate is one of the first things Vic and I learn how to make. Coco powder, sugar and milk, over a low flame and you have to stay with it, stirring it constantly. Hot chocolate mix? Haven't heard of it.

Hours. We spend hours, the four of us, sitting around the table focusing on a jigsaw puzzle. We might hardly have a word to say, except when one of us suddenly finds a piece we've been looking for. Then we might hoot. It can also be competitive, finding a piece you know someone else is hunting for and smugly pushing it into place right before their eyes. But otherwise it's quiet and soothing and contemplative. Hours sitting with my family in a tent, in the rain, so wonderfully peaceful.

When it's Yahtzee or a game of cards, it can be a whole different ballgame. There's strategy and skullduggery in these games and so there's a lot of hooting and name calling, and whoever happens to be the most clever at the moment gets to sit there and preen. Ha ha! Look at me and how smart I am! Playing Scrabble, dad is the most clever. He knows the strategy of waiting until just the right moment and if he has the Q's and the Z he'll hold onto them. Until... they fit into some obscure word no one else has ever heard of right on top of a red triple score. And cool as a cucumber, he adds them all up and does the math in his head and says, "That's... twenty-three... sixty-*nine* points." And if someone, which is usually me, can't stand it, and is willing to risk their next turn, they will challenge him and we get out the dictionary and find out he's right. And this person will sit and fume it out through his next turn. After a while we learn, and do not challenge him when he comes up with these blingers. But we then wonder... there is a chance he's pulling the wool over us.

When it rains for more than two days, a field trip to The Old Country Store in Moultonborough - been in business since 1781, ehya, dontcha knowit - is how we keep everyone sane. There are only so many hours, especially when you're seven or twelve, you can spend doing jigsaw puzzles.

Twisty country roads in New Hampshire, established hundreds of years back when the total sum of earth moving equipment was the pick and shovel and the peevee, go up and down with the landscape. "Peevee," by the way, is one of dad's favorite Scrabble words. The path of least resistance was as important then as now, and the old roads are fun and charming and beautiful. But, the constant change in pitch, yaw, and roll of the mighty Buick with mom, a.k.a. "Old Lead Foot," at the helm, is a recipe for motion sickness disaster.

I never want to admit I don't feel well, so instead of saying, "I don't feel well," I ask, "How long 'til we're there?"

"Oh, about a half hour," says mom, gassing it up the next hill.

I keep quiet. Anything more than two minutes of this seems like an eternity. I'll grin and bear it. I look out the window. I open the window and stick my nose out wishing for bus fumes but will settle for fresh air.

"It's raining dear, please close the window," says mom.

I close the window. The Buick is the first car we've had with electric windows and I've learned mom has switches to all of them, and a lock. So there's no arguing with her. I feel green. I feel greener. An excess of saliva forms in the back of my mouth. We launch over a rise and carve around a curve at the same time. I undo my seat belt and stand up and look out the windshield. Here comes another one. Ugh. Mom is intent, she powers through another curve.

"Mom?" I ask.

"Yes dear," she says.

"I don't..." And I flop back in my seat and Vic looks at me like 'what's wrong with you?' and I throw up on the floor. In a second the car fills with that smell. It's awful.

"Gordon threw up!" Yells Vic, oh, ugh, stating the blatantly obvious. "Gross! It's all over his feet and his flip-flops!" Thanks for pointing this out, Vic.

Mom looks for a place wide enough to pull off the road. And on these roads this can be miles away. So we go on, and on, and finally she says, "Here's a place to pull off the road." Oh yeah. The second we stop I get out. I want fresh air in the worst way, and so does everyone else. Mom comes around, and surveys the scene. It's not pretty. A situation like this is a test of a person's ability to be loving, and mom is admirably good natured.

"Sorry I got sick, mom," I say.

She puts her hand on top of my head. "Me too. It's ok, we'll get things cleaned up," she says. She gets some rags and a gallon jug of water from the trunk and cleans the carpet as best she can. I find a puddle in the ditch and go over to rinse my feet. I splash around for a minute before I realize I'm standing, bare legged, in a thicket of poison ivy.

There are moments in a boy's life which go beyond mere humiliation and this is one of them. I want to cry but instead keep my mouth shut, the 'be a young man' thing has already gotten into me. By the time we get to Moltonborough my feet and legs are covered with intensely itching flames of bright red blisters. I start scratching at the spots like a madman.

The Old Country Store is a happening place when it rains, a harbor of refuge for all the mothers in the lakes region trying to keep their sanity as best they can. The place is surrounded by cars, so we have to park way down the street. It's raining, pouring, I'm in my yellow plastic slicker and I pull the hood up. We get out of the car and start walking, me in a hobbly horse way, trying to walk and reach down to scratch my legs at the same time. Vic looks at me like 'you weirdo,' and then she realizes what's going on.

"How did you get poison ivy?" she asks right out loud, blowing my cover.

Mom looks at me. "Do you have poison ivy?" she asks. She looks me up and down and when she gets to my legs her face contorts in horror. "How did you get poison ivy?" she asks.

"When I rinsed my feet in the puddle," I say.

"Oh dear... *don't* touch it," she says. Yeah right. It's too late. Mom stops walking and thinks. "There's a pharmacy beside the grocery," she says. "Let's go there now and get some calamine lotion." She does an about face, and puts it in 'march.'

"But mom!" says Vic. "Aren't we going to The Old Country Store?"

"Yes dear," says mom, "but calamine lotion comes first." Vic sucks her teeth. When we get there mom says, "You two stay in the car. I'll only be a minute." We nod our wet straggly little red haired heads in unison. We could be so charming. When mom leaves I scratch at my legs.

"Don't touch it! Mom says!" says Vic.

"It's my poison ivy and I'll scratch it if I want!" I say.

"I'm going to tell mom!" says Vic.

"Don't!" I say. And we launch into a fight. We throw epithets at one another like 'you're dumb,' and 'you're a poop,' and snicker at one another until we see mom coming out of the pharmacy with a modest white bag. With the sight of her marching for the car, like turning a switch we are again two little angels.

Mom goes to work on my legs. "Have you been scratching it?" she asks.

"No," I say.

"Liar liar pants on fire!" says Vic. I glare at her and silently mouth 'you - are - going - to - get - it.' And I'd mouth '!' but there is no mouth for '!,' so I narrow my eyes and if I could coil up like a snake, I would.

Mom dabs calamine lotion onto my legs with cotton balls and some of the itching goes away. "Thanks mom," I say.

"You're welcome dear," she says and kisses me on the forehead. "When we get to The Old Country Store, first thing, I want you to go to the boy's room and wash your hands." She looks me in the eye to confirm.

"Yes, mom," I say. We get there and I hop out of the car. I look at my legs, two spindly white things sticking out from under a yellow rain slicker, all dabbed with pink polka dots, terminating in blue flip-flops. I can't wait for all the kids in there to see me, and more humiliation.

We step in the door and into a world of complete pandemonium. The place is packed with kid action, and clumps of damp harried moms standing on the sidelines. I am immediately drawn to the penny candy counter.

"Gordon?" It's the voice of authority coming from behind. "Do you remember what you are going to do first?" it asks.

I look at mom, already my gaze is filled with fruit slices and gummy bears. I pause. "Wash my hands?"

"Good. Then please go do that now," says mom. "There will still be plenty of candy when you get back." It takes every ounce of focus and determination I have to get to the men's room at the back of the store.

With my hands clean, I loiter for a while where they've built a beehive into the back window. You can watch the bees doing bee stuff inside the hive, it's a gooey sticky mess in there. But bees are cool.

I nudge into the back of the crowd at the penny candy counter which has grown exponentially since we arrived, and wait my turn. Anxiously I steal glimpses into the big glass case with all the candy in it. Two frazzled clerks are doing their best to take orders from kids. "I'd like three nonpareils, six Mary Janes, and, no, four nonpareils and four sour crawlers and four, no, two mint juleps, and…" For the clerks, making sense of this and keeping track, all while facing a crowd of twenty antsy children is Intro To Sainthood 101. They place the candies in small paper bags which are decorated with green and red stripes. They wipe the sweat from their brows, asking, "Anything else?" hoping and praying the kid will shake their head, "no." They then guide their young customer to the giant old mechanical cash register with the numbers that pop up and down behind a glass window on top, and close the deal. Finally it's my turn and before I know it, the 50¢ mom gave me is used up and I have a bag full of colorful, wonderful sweet treats.

Mom is doing her own shopping. She gets a bag of horehounds for her and dad. Why anyone would willingly eat something that tastes like cough syrup is beyond me. She also gets a few sour dill pickles from the barrel and a wedge of rat cheese. The pickles are so sour your mouth turns inside out when you eat one, which makes them kinda fun, and the rat cheese, well... Everyone else calls this sharp cheddar but we call it rat cheese because it is so smelly and sharp only a rat would eat it. Why buy it then, one might wonder? It is *the* secret ingredient in macaroni and cheese. There is nothing, *nothing!*, as good as mom's macaroni and cheese made with rat cheese. Mom also gets a bar of blueberry soap, a treat for her and Vic. It's a luscious deep blue and smells so strongly of blueberries I only want to eat it, but mom assures me this is not a good idea. Why anyone would want to wash and end up smelling like a blueberry... I guess you need to be a girl to understand this.

With my bag of candy closely in hand I wander around the store. They have a player guitar. Like a player piano, it runs off a paper scroll, but has a mechanism that plucks the strings. It actually works, someone puts a nickel in it and off it goes. It's a crazy thing to watch.

It's time to go back to Robies, so we gather up our goodies and step out onto the front porch. The rain is coming down in buckets, sheets of water drift across the road. Big rain drops hitting puddles and these rivulets send out ripples and make bubbles. A "frog chokin' gulley washer," as Uncle Mike says. We make a run for the car and clamor in, now soaked. Mom turns on the air. It helps clear the windows, but, "Mom, it's freezing in here," I say.

"Where's the car blanket?" she asks. "Isn't it back there?"

"Yes," I say.

"Why don't you wrap up in it?" she asks, adding, "I'll only run the air for a few minutes."

"O.K.," I say.

Vic and I look at each other. Vic whispers, "...run the air..." and we snicker. We huddle together under the itchy wool blanket and warm up. It's pretty clammy, but at least we're warm. We're flying along, and studying and eating the contents of our candy bags. Suddenly mom brakes the car. We look up.

We're in Melvin Village just past the Hansel and Gretel Shop. This is a nice enough little town, but they've cleverly posted a speed limit greatly reduced from the approaching road and they have a speed cop who takes the enforcement of the speed limit very seriously. This is his job, an important one, to make the village safe so they say. We think it's all about plumping up the town coffers. At least mom a.k.a. "Old Lead Foot" thinks so. Mom hisses, "there's the town cop!" We're all hoping and praying he stays right where he is, as we slink by. Mom keeps a beady eye on her rear view mirror once we've passed. Vic and I peer out the back window. No speed cop. When we go around the bend and out of view mom steps on it, and the old Buick's afterburners kick in and we're gonzo. Perhaps sugar is an effective preventative for motion sickness - we make it back to Wolfeboro and I feel fine. Will have to tell mom about this new benefit of sugar before the next road trip.

Anytime between Memorial Day and Labor Day, downtown Wolfeboro is a snarl of traffic, and especially so when it rains. The rest of the year, Main Street is a nice place to lay down and take a nap. But on this soggy afternoon, summer folks in their slickers are all over the place. Bradley's Hardware and Hunter's Market are especially hard hit, and good places to save for another time. Nonetheless, mom asks, "how about a few ears of corn to go with dinner?" Vic and I look at each other and silently acknowledge this question is merely a thin guise for the statement, "We're stopping at Hunters," with a smirk.

Resistance is useless. Mom already has her blinker on and we wait for an eternity to cross traffic into the parking lot. Half an opportunity presents itself and mom says, "Step on it boy," and she does step on it and we burst in front of an oncoming car, the driver of which is not exactly pleased, fly into the lot and then jam on the brakes to avoid hitting the car in front of us. Now it's a matter of circling until a space opens - kind of like the holding pattern at O'Hare, but fraught with more anxiety. This takes a while. When we finally have a place to park mom turns to us. "You two want to stay here or come with me?" she asks.

Vic looks at me and I look at Vic with about as much enthusiasm for this as getting a filling. "We'll stay here," says Vic.

"Suit yourselves," says mom and she heads for the store. We get back into our candy bags. Little do we know, fillings are in our futures.

I've decided mint juleps are not my favorite. I ask Vic, "Do you have any fruit slices?"

"Yes," she says. She looks at me suspiciously, which is warranted.

"I'll trade you my mint juleps, even. I have three," I say.

"What's the matter with the mint juleps?" she asks. She's on to me.

"Nothing," I say. "You want to trade?"

"Nope," she says.

I look in my bag and consider my trading options. "Three mint juleps and one Boston baked bean for two fruit slices?" I ask. I really want to get rid of those mint juleps.

"Nope." Vic ponders this for a moment and adds, "Throw in a caramel and I'll trade."

"Deal," I say. Vic is smarter in business than me.

"There's mom," says Vic. "Just wait, she's going to…"

Mom jumps in the car and throws a soggy paper bag that's falling apart on the passenger seat. "Two dollars for a dozen ears of corn!" she squawks. "Robbery! I'll never…" But we do go back to Hunter's, and the prices never go down.

. . .

During those long periods of darkness in Concord a.k.a. "the school year," we make frequent trips to Haggett's. While mom considers the latest in Coleman stoves or picks up a few packages of replacement mantles for the lantern, I study the fishing tackle. It is said fishing tackle is designed as much to catch fishermen as fish. From my experience, with only a few exceptions, I have found this to be true. Especially with regard to lures.

These devices couldn't be more appropriately named. I gaze at the displays in the store and I have cash in my pocket from doing my chores. The lures are brilliant, plated with shiny metals, painted bright colors, spinners, spoons and poppers, jigs, buzz baits and plugs. Some are beaded, some have feathers. All have hooks. Most are available in a range of sizes, the variations on the theme are endless. And the way they work - usually not very well - presents a strong case fish are smarter than fishermen.

The fisherman first considers the fish he hopes to catch and then his options in lures. Say he has a small mouth bass in mind, a real fighting fish that frequents rocky shoals in open water of the local lakes. He will anchor the boat and cast, he may troll. The small mouth bass is larger than a smelt and smaller than a yellow fin tuna so the lure must be the appropriate size. He goes to his sporting goods shop and gazes at the displays and while doing his best to think like a hungry small mouth bass, makes his choice, or better yet, choices. Best to be prepared. And he forks over his hard earned cash.

He goes fishing, he's out there at the right time of day, he's out there for hours, he tries a few different spots, he casts, he trolls, he uses alternative lures. The lures whiz through the water, they wobble and flash and spin. And the fish are there and simply watch them go by.

"Charlie, will you look at that buzz bait!"

"Jeesch! You've got to be kidding me..."

They consider their options and decide to give this thing a pass. Perhaps some minnows, a wayward crawdad or maybe a stranded dragonfly for breakfast, but not a buzz bait.

When we return to Robie's we discover we have new neighbors, the Scotts. They have their small trailer in the other primo spot. It's a knoll overlooking the marsh and while they're further from the beach than us, they have *the* view of the lake. I immediately become friends with Mr. Scott who after a short time insists I call him Harvey. "Yes Mr. Scott, I mean Harvey," I say. Harvey is a fisherman, and now that he's retired from many years at the G.E. plant in Lynn, he lives to be out on the water and fish.

With the demands of supporting the family, my dad isn't around much, and with his distant nature, when he is around he wasn't often engaged with us. Sad, in a way. As a boy growing up, I am craving some man energy, and so have a number of men friends who become mentors, and Harvey is the first. He has a kind nature and a soft, deeply lined face; right off I take a shine to him and he to me. We become fishing buddies and he lets me use one of his rods with an open face spinning reel.

First off I need to learn to cast. Harvey sets me up on the shore near the shuffle board. It's sandy and open and because the slope into the water is steep no one swims here. "Always look at what's behind you before bringing the rod back to cast," says Harvey. He tells me a story of the fisherman who doesn't look and swings his rod back and catches his friend in the ear with the hook and then whips the rod forward. Before anyone knows what's happening he rips his friend's ear clean off his head. The horror! So Harvey helps me get the hang of it and every time he says, "Look behind you." Eventually, I do. Every time. And Harvey says, "Good. I consider my ears safe."

To make a cast with an open face spinning reel the bail which spins and holds the line on the spool is drawn back and the fisherman holds the line with the tip of his index finger. He looks behind him, draws the rod back and with some oomph, whips it forward and at just the right moment lets go of the line and zzzing! Off goes the lure, flying gracefully through the air, pulling out the line with it and plop! It falls exactly where he wants. Exactly where that bass, he knows it, is lurking. The fisherman cranks the reel, the bail snaps over the line capturing it and winds it in. Well, this is what happens when the fisherman knows what he's doing, which is something I do not.

I'm standing at the water's edge, I look behind me, the coast is clear, then release the bail and forget I need to catch the line with my finger tip. Plop. The lure falls, limp, into the water. Ok, I reel the lure in a bit, we'll start again. I look behind me, the coast is still clear, grip the line, release the bail, swing the rod back, whip it forward and release the line. But I release it at the wrong moment and the lure goes flying about 60 degrees off to the right, far, far away from the direction of that magical fish infested place. Harvey chuckles and patiently explains what I need to do differently.

When he's confident I have the gist of it, he leaves me to my own devices. "You practice for a while. You'll figure it out," he says. He gives my butch haircut a scruffing. I stand there and practice and when I think I'm getting the hang of it, zzzing! the lure shoots off to the right or left. If there's anyone around when this happens I quickly turn in that direction, hoping it looks like I intended the lure to go that way from the start. I hear laughter and turn around. It's Harvey, walking around the point and wagging a finger at me. "I saw that!" he says. I grin sheepishly and shrug my shoulders. He comes over and gives me a few tips.

I keep at it. As my casts improve my confidence builds. Vic comes by.

"How's it going, " she asks.

"Good. Watch this," I say. I look behind me and cast and this time, I have an audience after all, I give it a good whip and zzzing! The lure shoots into space, it's going exactly in the direction I want, straight across the channel. The delicate monofilament line flies off the spool, and I'm thinking this must be very impressive to my sister. And, and, the lure falls, but there is no plop. What? Um? I start to crank in the line. Vic's standing there, watching. The line goes taught and this is when it becomes apparent the lure is caught in the bushes on the other side of the channel.

"Show off," says Vic.

I give the line a tug but this just sets the hook deeper into whatever branch it's caught in. Vic starts to walk away. "Hey, wait a minute," I say. "Could you help me? I don't want to lose Harvey's lure." Vic stops and looks at me. That knowing look. Knowing she is getting sucked into something it's probably not a good idea to get sucked into.

"How?" she asks, not exactly brimming with enthusiasm.

"Could you row over there and get the lure out of the bushes?" The corners of Vic's mouth visibly droop. "I'll get you six nonpareils the next time we go to The Old Country Store," I say. Vic flutters her eyebrows with the slightest hint of interest. I'm at her mercy. No way can I leave Harvey's rod and reel in the sand and do this all by myself. "Please?" I ask.

"Deal," she says. "But you better not forget about the nonpareils."

"I promise," I say. I always give away the farm, and reconsider she probably would have done it for four. But now it's too late. Vic goes over to the rowboats and unties and pushes one in the water, and I'm relieved and hope Harvey doesn't come along. Vic rows into the channel and has difficulty seeing the line. In the air it's all but invisible. She finds it and following it points the bow of the boat into the bushes. Twigs and branches squeak as they rub against the aluminum hull. Vic stows the oars and gets up, but when she walks forward in the boat, it slips backward out of the bushes, far enough the offending branch is out of her reach. The current starts the boat drifting downstream. She tries again with the same result. "Row really hard into the bushes!" I yell. "Ramming speed!"

She looks at me as though she's wondering how and why she got herself into this pickle. I worry she's going to row back and call it a day, which would not be at all unreasonable. But she rows into the channel, aims the boat for the place in the bushes and gives it everything her thirteen year old kid girl body's got. "My hero!" I shout. And the boat smashes into the bushes, the bow lifts out of the water, twigs screaming and scratching all the way. She quickly stows the oars and hops to the bow and grabs a branch. Holding the branch with one hand she searches for the line. She finds it and follows it, and there's the lure! Red and white and twinkly.

"Vic! Here comes a boat!" I yell. It's Mr. and Mrs. Walker in Mr. Walker's old race boat. It's a low and slinky and scary thing in the water. They're coming in from the lake, but going slow.

"Don't tug on the line!" shouts Vic. "Let it go loose and don't pull on it until I say so!"

"O.K.!" I shout. Vic is fumbling with her one free hand, untangling the line and freeing the lure. I wave to the Walker's and make a motion for them to stop. Mr. Walker can see something's going on, so he waves and stops and waits. The engine on the race boat clatters at idle, the boat drifts a bit backwards.

"I got it!" yells Vic. She tosses the lure into the water. "O.K., now reel it in."

I start cranking the line in fast. The lures comes flitting across the channel, wildly popping out of the water then diving. I get it in and wave to the Walkers. Mr. Walker lifts a horn into the air and gives it a blast and grins devilishly as he motors by. They all wave and say hello and continue to their dock. The race boat is the wildest looking thing I've ever seen.

Vic gets back. "Thanks Vic," I say. "You're my hero." She smiles. "And I won't forget about the nonpareils. Six of them."

. . .

Harvey has a ten foot pram made of crinkly aluminum, with a little outboard motor on it. Mom and dad talk with him and agree it will be O.K. for me to go out on the lake with him. In these discussions, Harvey looks at me and says, "You have to be able to swim around the boat. Can you do that?" What being able to swim around a boat has to do with being able to handle yourself if you get thrown overboard is unclear to me, yet it is the standard and time honored test.

I look at mom and dad. Mom smiles, dad just stands there. I pivot my toe in the dirt. "I guess so," I say.

"Well then, let's find out," says Harvey. We all go to where his boat is pulled up. This is not beach, it's just marshy shore, and the bottom is black, all muck and slime. Harvey and I push out a few feet in the boat. "Well. Jump in, let's see what you can do. I won't go anywhere," he says. Mom and dad are watching expectantly from shore. I stand up, pull off my t-shirt, hold my nose and do a cannon ball into the water. My feet just touch bottom. Under water I am momentarily surrounded with sounds of bubbles swirling around. Like a cork, I pop up and start dog paddling like my life depends on it. What does depend on it - going fishing with Harvey - is just as important. And I dog paddle around the boat and when I finish, grab ahold of the gunnel and rest and everyone hoots and claps and I am one happy kid.

At first light the next morning, Harvey and I head out onto the lake. It's unusual for me to be up this early, everyone else in the tent is asleep, so I grab a cruller and a paper cup of milk and sit outside. It's grey and still and chilly, I peer across the lake, it's perfectly calm. The campground is quiet, even the *skrikas* are asleep. I'm still groggy when I show up at the Scott's trailer, greeted by smells of bacon and coffee in the air. Harvey is cooking breakfast on his camp stove under the tarp. He sees me ambling up. "Good morning," he says in a hushed voice. "Have you had breakfast?"

"Yep," I say, gazing at the strips of bacon sputtering around in the skillet. The smell of frying bacon, when I'm hungry is almost unbearable. Maybe I'm drooling, my stomach growls.

"Was that you?" asks Harvey.

"I didn't say anything," I reply.

"But your stomach did," he says. "Sure you wouldn't like some bacon and eggs?" When my eyes meet his I can't help but smile. "Good," he says. "We're going to be on the water for a while. A fisherman needs a proper breakfast so he can concentrate on catching fish." We sit at Harvey's picnic table, the sky brightens bit by bit. He fixes me up with a paper plate with two eggs sunny side up and three strips of bacon and a slice of bread. "No toaster," he says. "We're roughing it." Bacon fat soaks into my paper plate, making it translucent. He pours me a cup of orange juice. We sit and eat and Harvey gives me the details,

"We'll fish at the ledges between Mink and Brummet islands and we'll start out with night crawlers. All the lures in the world, there's nothing like a crawler for catching bass." Harvey is itching to go, we finish breakfast, I gather every last bit of the gleaming yellow egg yolk off my plate with my fork, and scrape it clean with my teeth then help Harvey clean up.

Harvey has all our tackle set aside. We divvy it up and head for the boat. The lake is smooth as glass. Amazing, such a big body of water can be so still. Not a ripple. The lone bullfrog croaking goes silent when we clamor around the boat. After getting everything situated, we push off. Harvey takes his seat in the stern and I sit in the bow. The motor, a Johnson 3 h.p., is completely self contained with a fuel tank built into the top of its housing. Harvey unscrews the gas cap and tops up the fuel from the two gallon can he brings along. After securing the cap he fiddles with the choke and throttle and pulls on the starter cord and the motor pops to life. There's no neutral or gear shift, so when the motor starts, right away, it propels the boat, only problem is we're only twenty feet away from shore and now at a good clip, headed directly for it. This isn't looking like a smooth start, but for Harvey it's part of the routine. He deftly pivots the motor 180 degrees around on it's mount and presto! We're going in reverse. We back away from shore a ways and Harvey then pivots the motor back and steers us out toward open water.

We putter out of the cove leaving a trail of bubbles in the calm water, and a long low cloud of oily blue smoke in the equally calm air. We pass thickets of lily pads and long wavy tendrils of water grass. The water is dark, but then quickly becomes light as we pass over the sandbar at the mouth of the cove. As suddenly again we are over deep water and Harvey opens up the throttle. This is the first time I've been out on the lake. The view opens up around us. Granted when you're small everything looks big, but the sweep of open water and space is vast, I've never seen anything like it. The boat buzzes and reverberates tingly vibrations from the motor as we plough along. We head in an easterly direction, and I have a funny feeling being in such deep water, that if somehow the water were to disappear we would be left in mid-air, we would fall fifty, sixty feet to the bottom. Not to mention if I were swimming, I couldn't touch the bottom. This occupies my mind uneasily and I tighten my grip on the gunnels. Harvey must be picking up on it. He steers the tiller a bit side to side and we tip this way and that in a zigzag course. He shouts over the buzzing, "Having fun?"

I manage a smile and nod my head - not quite sure of this, but it is fun. I look behind us, our wake is a silly curvy thing stretching across the water. We head into the sunrise, in a few minutes the sun will be fully over the horizon and this is a good thing. The morning air hugging the water is damp and cold and I'm starting to shake with the chills. With the sun comes some warmth. We navigate between Mink and Stamp Act islands and slow down. From the surface nothing looks different, but Harvey knows we're coming up on the ledges. Going slower, the buzzing in the hull goes away and I can hear myself think. Now we can see the bottom, rocks and boulders strewn about, all covered with a light brown-green coating of algae. The water is only a few feet deep in places. "I'll bet these rocks have gobbled up some boats in the middle of the night," says Harvey. "And probably a few in broad daylight!" We circle around. "Why don't you get ready to set the anchor when I say so," he says. "First, please make sure the bitter-end of the rope is tied to the boat!" He looks at me with wide eyes and laughs.

I study the anchor, which looks like a giant silver mushroom and figure out the rope. It's in a loose heap and tied to a bracket in the bow. Harvey slows the motor so we're barely putting along. "Prepare to make anchor," he says, then adds, "Don't throw it in, let it slip quietly over the gunnel." I get ready and when Harvey says, "Anchor away!" I heft the heavy thing up and place it overboard and slowly feed out the rope until it hits bottom. "First class," says Harvey and he shuts down the motor. Suddenly all becomes peaceful. We drift, the anchor rope plays out knocking softly against the gunnel. It is the only sound. We survey our surroundings. "Beautiful isn't it?" asks Harvey in a low voice.

"Sure is, " I say. "We're the first on the lake."

"First come, first served," says Harvey, glancing toward the water and grinning. "Let's fish." We come to the end of the anchor line and the boat gently swings around against it. Harvey has already set up the two rods with hooks and sinkers and bobbers. He moves slowly and quietly in the boat and hands me the rod I've been using for practice. Now however, this is the real thing. I might even catch a fish. "Do you know how to bait a hook?" asks Harvey.

"No," I say, feeling a little embarrassed. Casting is the extent of my skill, and it's only the beginning.

"Well, now you're going to learn, " he says. "Take the tension off your line and free the hook from the guide." This much I know how to do. Harvey hands me a coffee can. "Now dig in there and find yourself a big fat crawler." The can is half full of rich black soil and not a worm in sight. Noticing I'm not getting very far with finding a crawler he says, "You have to dig for them." I plunge my fingers deeper into the soil and am met with the feeling of cold damp snakes curling around my fingers. I look at Harvey, full of apprehension. "Grab one and pull it out, they don't bite" he says, encouraging me on and laughing. I pull out a night crawler, it's fat and writhes all around. "You don't need a whole one on your hook. Pinch it in half and give one half to me," he says.

"Pinch it in half?" I don't like the idea of this at all, and hope an SPCA special agent isn't parked on shore watching this with his binoculars.

"Go ahead," Harvey urges, "he's going to get eaten by a fish in a few minutes, anyway."

I take a deep breath, wince, and pinch the night crawler in half. I'm not enjoying this, and clearly the night crawler is not enjoying this either. I hand one half to Harvey. "Thanks," he says. "Watch me bait my hook, then you do yours." I'm holding the madly twisting half of night crawler in my hand, and watch Harvey place his over the hook and then hooking it again, and again so the crawler is now a thoroughly impaled curlicue. "There," he says, satisfied. "This way the fish can't just nibble the bait off the hook. They're clever that way. But this one, he'll have to take the whole thing in his mouth. Got it?" he asks.

"Yes," I say.

"Well, go ahead and bait your hook," he says. I find out it's not as easy as it looks. The half of crawler still has enough sense to not be going for this. "Be careful not to hook yourself," adds Harvey. I persevere, and finally get the poor thing on the hook. "Good work," he says, "now, figure out where you want to cast, look behind you and let'r fly!"

Being the thinking boy, I decide to cast downwind. I check behind, no, there's no one there, no ears to catch, and I release the bail, hold the line with my finger and bring the rod back. I whip it forward and the hook and sinker and bobber, and the half crawler go flying through the air, the crawler to meet it's ultimate doom, and the whole kit arcs down gracefully and plop!, hits the water. Amazing.

"Take a turn on the crank," says Harvey, "so your line's secure. You never know when a fish is going to strike your hook. Watch your bobber."

I follow his prompt. And now I am fishing. I watch Harvey cast his line. His actions are measured and certain. Even though he's casting upwind his setup goes twice the distance of mine. I'm impressed, more, in awe.

And so we sit. With a light breeze coming up, small waves lap against the hull, a few other boats appear on the water, and the climbing sun warms us up. Harvey keeps his eye on his bobber; me, I'm daydreaming about something… and all of a sudden Harvey pulls back on his pole, seems he has a fish and he's setting the hook. The pole bends and quivers in a graceful arc. The line dances this way and that. The drag on his reel releases with the pull of the fish. I watch him crank in the line and then wait. Harvey glances at me. "Pay attention to your bobber," he says. "This fish might have his friends along with him." My bobber is having a merry time, floating, but not bobbing. Then there's a quiver, the bobber dips ever so slightly under the surface. I wildly yank back on my pole, it must be a whale! But the bobber and hook come popping out of the water with no fish. "You don't want to pull the whole thing out of his mouth, " says Harvey as he plays his fish. "You want him to get the hook fully in his mouth and then set it with a tug. You'll get it." I crank in my line and watch Harvey. The fish he's got is tiring and he brings it in close to the boat. "It's a white perch, pretty good size. We'll keep him," he says. "Would you hand me the net?"

I hand it to him. With one hand holding his rod, which now has quite a bend to it, he lifts and gets the fish right by the boat and he scoops him up from behind. Harvey wets his hand, then slips it over the fish from nose to tail, folding its dorsal fin back so he won't get stabbed by the spines protruding from the top edge. He uses a pair of needle nose pliers to remove the hook from the fish's mouth. "He's a nice one, about ten inches," he says. This perch, like all fish, is made for the water, its body a teardrop shape and coloring like the lake bottom, an earthy green. Harvey puts the fish on the stringer and puts him in the water. "Let's freshen our bait and find another one," he says. We go through the night crawler routine again. Baiting the hook is a part of fishing I never quite warm up to. Maybe lures, if you can actually catch a fish with one, aren't such bad ideas. We cast and start the process anew.

There's a lot of sitting around with fishing, the lack of activity is something I'm not accustomed to. Harvey and I talk about fishing and fish and boats and motors. And I fidget. This being peaceful thing is a new concept. After a while I get accustomed to it and become more quiet and look at the lake and shore.

And whammo! Out of this blissful scene, my bobber plunges underwater and doesn't come up, the drag on my reel releases and buzzes like a swarm of killer bees. "Hold on Gordon, you've got a great white shark on there!" hollers Harvey. I am taken completely off guard and my heart is racing. The line rushes out, my rod is bending, I don't know what to do and plaintively look at Harvey. "Tighten the drag... that's the knob on the front of the spool... just a little bit," he says. "You don't want him to run forever, but you don't want to break the line either." So I tighten the drag, and the line slows... and slows a bit more and then stops releasing. "He's taking a breather," says Harvey.

"Keep the tip of your rod up, not too far... crank him in a bit... keep a tension on him..."

We two are completely focused on this leviathan on my line. It's slow going. "I bet it's a bass," says Harvey, "the way he's fighting." I glance at him and smile. Small mouth bass are the prize fish in this lake, I'm excited and don't want to screw it up. Suddenly, the drag on Harvey's reel starts screaming.

"You've got one too!" I shout. Harvey grabs his rod and starts playing the fish.

"This is a big one... I got my hands full," he blurts out. "Keep a tension on him... work him in..." There's a certain amount of grunting and hooting and the boat lurches one way and the other as we keep tension in our lines. It's tempting to stand up, but with the two of us in such a small boat there's a danger of tipping the thing over. We also need to keep our lines from crossing, which could make things very confusing very quickly. I am entranced with the energy of the fish on the line and get my first bittersweet taste of a living thing struggling, against me, for its life.

Harvey's fish breaks the surface, flying into the air, arcing its body in an effort to dislodge the hook from its mouth. It's a good size bass. It dives and breaks again and comes off the hook. "Lost him!" shouts Harvey. "Too bad. I was thinking he'd make me a nice dinner," and he laughs. "Now it's up to you." The fish on my line is tiring. Harvey waits to see how things will go for me before setting up his tackle. Eventually I bring the fish in close to the boat. It's a bass, not the biggest, but big enough to keep. "You bring him around in my direction and I'll net him," says Harvey. We jostle around, and Harvey nets the fish. He directs me how to hold it and hands me the pliers to pull the hook. I have a firm grasp on the fish and reach into his mouth and remove the hook. Free of it the bass lurches violently and in my surprise I let go. He flips and flops around in the boat. "He might jump out!" exclaims Harvey, and we both jump to grab the fish but it's too quick. The boat rocks. Harvey grabs the net and tosses it on the fish. "Got him... they'll jump right out of the boat if you don't watch out," he says. I free the bass from the net and we put him alongside Harvey's perch on the stringer.

We continue to fish the ledges until close to noon and catch a half-dozen or so perch and bass. A moderate chop has come up and the sun is high. Every exposed part of me, which is most, is turning bright red. In the typical burn and peel cycle, of which tan is not part of the picture. "Time to head in," says Harvey. "When the light's too bright, the fish head for the shadows." He pulls the stringer into the boat. We've caught four perch and three bass. None may be prize fish by the usual measures, but all are to me.

I pull the anchor and Harvey starts the motor and off we go. The boat creaks and twists in the waves. We joke about it being made of recycled beer cans, but more likely made from recycled war planes. Who knows. Water splashes over the bow and I get soaked. This is not cause for complaint, it feels good, and when we get back, this will fit right in with the tales of high seas adventure I want to tell.

Mom and dad and Vic are duly impressed with my catch. "We need to clean them," says mom. "Seems this is something, being a fisherman, you need to learn. Come along. I'll clean these and you watch." We walk over to the fish table with me toting the fish on a string. Mom has her hunting knife and a whetstone. She takes the knife out of the sheath, it's just right for her small hands and inspects the edge by dragging her thumb cross-wise over it. The handle is burl wood with an s-curve steel hilt. "Could use a little touch-up," she says and gives the blade a few licks on the stone. I watch her intently. "You need a sharp knife to clean fish. We're all set."

"Mom, it was so calm on the lake this morning, and then the waves came up," I say. "I like being out on the lake. It's kind of scary, it's so dark and deep, but I like it. It's so big!"

"*I'd* like it if you learned to swim better," she says.

"I dog paddled around the boat!" I remind her.

"Shore can be a long swim away," she says. I realize she has a point. "We'll teach you the crawl. You're big enough now to do it. Let's clean these fish."

Mom takes one of the perch, and promptly cuts the head off just behind the gills. Her actions with the knife are precise and efficient. She cuts the belly open and with her fingers pushes out the entrails. "Want to see what it was eating?" she asks. I nod my head dubiously. With the tip of the knife she pricks open the stomach. A little blob of bugs and a few minnows and a piece of night crawler fall out. She points to the crawler, saying, "there's his last meal." This gives me something to think about, life and death, and the business of killing. She cuts off the tail, makes an incision along the back and pulls off the skin. "There," she says. "We'll rinse it off, and it will be ready to cook." In no time she has my catch cleaned. "Next time you'll clean your own fish," she says matter-of-factly.

We're hosing off the table and Harvey walks over. "Elna, you've got quite a fisherman on your hands here," he says. I feel about as proud as a kid can. "No more trips to the fish market for you."

Mom smiles. "Thanks for taking Gordon out. It means a lot to him," she says. "And we're happy to have the fish."

Later, I help mom cook dinner. We bread the fish in cornmeal and flour, and fry them in butter in a cast iron skillet over the fire. They'll be our main course, the taste is of deep water from the lake, clean, fresh and sweet. The taste is especially sweet for me.

In campgrounds nearly everyone hangs a sign in front of their setup with their name and home town painted on it. Like wearing a name tag at a convention, the signs are ice breakers and an invitation to stop and have a little talk. For the first couple of summers at Robies we didn't have one, but one evening dad shows up with a sign he painted at home. It's a small wooden yoke, just like what you'd put around the necks of oxen and hanging from the two hoops is the sign which he hand painted with "*THE BUNKERS* Concord, New Hampshire," in neat draftsmanship, with drop shadows no less. Between the two hoops hangs a decorative gold plated ring. I am fascinated that the ring is made of plastic but somehow looks like gold. Like fishing lures, I'm attracted to whatever is shiny and bright.

Campers are a friendly bunch and they wander around, say hello and loiter. In the evenings, this usually includes sitting around someone's campfire and the grown-ups get into the beer and wine. These gatherings and the ruckus they create draw even more campers and swarms of kids, until with no effort on the part of the host, who didn't even know he was going to be one, there's a full-blown party going on at his campsite. Often the festivities go late into the night. One such bash gets into full swing at a campsite near the shuffleboard court. People show up with lawn chairs, and a large crowd of grown-ups accumulates around the fire. The stories and laughter circle around and kids swoop in and out. In our excitement we run flat out, chasing and catching and being caught and all the while screaming our lungs out. Wild peccaries have nothing on us. It is as though our bare feet have eyes that can see in the dark. We run in the woods with roots and stumps and rocks, we fly, stubbed toe free. We come back to the party, panting, leaning on one parent or the other in their lawn chairs. They tell us to slow down and we never do. Once we catch our breath, we dash off into the darkness for more adventure.

The hosts of this particular shindig have their station wagon parked nearby. The back window is open and a small dog pokes his head out, keeping track of the goings on and no doubt interested in the smells of fatty meats grilling on the fire. It's a dachshund, a cute little fellow with bright beady eyes, and I walk right up to give him a pat. With the speed of a lightning strike, GROWL-*BITE!* He gives me a good snap, opening up the side of my right thumb. I let out a scream, as much from the surprise as the wound, which creates instant confusion and upset around the fire, the grown-ups jumping up from their lawn chairs, suddenly feeling the effects of too many beers. Chairs go flying, grown-ups bump into one another, they get their bearings and come running to this kid who shrieks like he's mortally wounded, but no, he only has a thumb torn apart.

Mom takes me back to our campsite. It's quiet and I calm down and she cleans and dresses the wound, and tells me I need to be careful around dogs I don't know. No drama, no lawsuits. Just be careful.

This experience is the start of 40 years of being scared witless of dachshunds. I've crossed the street to avoid sharing a sidewalk with one of the little terrors. This changes, however, when years later I am thrown into close proximity with one on a construction site. His name is Max. With 40 years of life under my belt I begin to understand why dachshunds are so aggressive. I would be too if I had legs three inches long and was surrounded by giants towering nine times my height. Max is the homeowner's dog and the homeowner is on site and Max is a holy four legged rapscallion varmint assault weapon. Every morning I show up, it's time to get the crew together and motivated to actually get some work done and Max launches out his micro dog door, his legs are a blur. He charges me, taunts, snaps, barks and growls and when I try to get away from him he has the nerve to keep after me with more.

I consider bringing a snake handling stick - the kind animal patrol would use to pick up a rattler - and placing him in the dumpster with it. But, I happen to like the homeowner and he is, after all, the person who signs the checks. So Max and I go through this dance, and while I begin to see it's all an act, I look at the scar on my thumb and recite the backwoods saying used to calculate the risk of getting attacked by a grizzly bear (and other wild animals including dachshunds), "never say never."

About midway though the project the homeowner gets a job in town so he is now absent from the site. And *just like that*, Max becomes my best friend. I show up in the morning and he launches out his dog door, tail wagging, he's jumping and running around me and rolls over on his back and I scratch his belly and he's in-between my feet. All day he's my little shadow. Max and I become great buddies. Funny, the things in life it takes 40 years to figure out, and now thanks to Max, dachshunds are my favorite dogs. I just love 'em.

. . .

The sandbar at the mouth of the cove is the coolest thing. Just when you think you're headed for deep water, up comes the bottom and it's beautiful nearly white sand, and it's shallow enough for swimming. If I were more easily persuaded by my impulses, I'd rightly jump out of the boat every time we go over it, it's that inviting.

Bless old Robie's heart for creating the campground beach, but once the idea of swimming at the sandbar lodges in my brain, it holds little appeal. If you like muck, bloodsuckers and on a busy day a very high concentration of urine, it's fine. But if you don't, and finding a bloodsucker under your bathing suit firmly attached to your butt will put you there in a hurry, you ask mom something like, "Could Vic and I row one of the boats out to the sandbar to go swimming?"

Mom thinks about this for a moment, and smartly says, "why don't I come out with you, the first time or two at least?" As the mom, she has concern for her progeny's safety and well-being. But who knows how many bloodsuckers she's found under her own bathing suit lately? So we happily agree to her terms and get Pamp to outfit one of the boats with an anchor. In the true spirit of making something materialize out of nothing, it's a jumbo tomato sauce can filled with cement, with a bent-over hoop of steel re-bar cast into it, tied onto a hank of bristly jute rope. It's not pretty but it works.

Out we go, Vic, mom and me. I've grown enough to handle the oars and quickly discover rowing a boat to the sandbar, as opposed to having Harvey's 3 h.p. motor get us there, is a lot of work. By the time we get there I'm pooped and have a couple of blisters on the palms of my hands. Still, we're having a good time, rowing into the big water. We find a suitable spot to make anchor. Mom's about to throw the anchor overboard and I say, "make sure the other end of the rope is tied to the boat!" She gives me a slightly irritated look. "Harvey taught me," I say. Mom fumbles through the mess of rope and finds it's not tied. I do my best not to look smug. She ties it off to the bow eye, using the Boy Scout method: if you don't know the right knot to tie, tie a lot of them.

Faced with a whole lake full of clear water, and not knowing how deep it is, I use an oar as a measuring stick. I push it down into the water until the tip hits bottom. It then bobs up, I lift it the rest of the way into the boat and hold it beside me. Jumping into all this expanse of water and having it above my head would be too much. To my relief, the wet line comes up to my chest, so I peel off my t-shirt and stand on the middle bench seat and jump in. The boat rocks wildly, Vic and mom hoot. I'm in the water and dog paddling and it isn't more than a minute before they jump in.

There's a light chop and the waves splash over my head and slap against me. The open water is a wild place compared to the protected campground beach. But the sand is clean, the water is fresh and clear and there's no muck, no yuk. We're splashing around, it's heavenly.

"Maybe this is a good time to learn the crawl," says mom. This is actually the *Australian* Crawl, and I was afraid she was going to mention this. I've watched mom and Vic do it and it looks way too complicated. Without waiting to hear whether I'm into this or not, mom says, "Here, let me hold you from underneath." She scooches down and sticks her arms out. "You lay on my arms." This is all a little bit awkward, and I crane my neck to hold my head above water. "No dear, when you do the crawl you're supposed to keep your head down."

"But mom, if I keep my head down, I'll drown," I say. Already I'm completely not into this.

"You rotate your head, watch me," she says and she lets go of me. I flub around for a second and get my footing. Mom stands and bends over so her torso is in the water. She puts her head underwater and looks down and blows bubbles. Then she rotates her head to the side. When her mouth is out of water, she takes in a breath. She repeats this a few times and stands up. "See?" she asks. "That's how you keep your head down and breathe."

"I see… mom I'm getting cold," I say. Already I want this lesson to be over.

"Just give it a try," she says and demonstrates again.

I bend over like she does. I blow bubbles under water like she does. I rotate my head like she does, and when I open my mouth to take a breath a wave comes rolling along and swamps me and I inhale a mouthful of water. I immediately stand up choking, and cough and spit.

"You need to have your head above water before you take a breath," she says. I love it when I'm screwing up and someone states the blatantly obvious. "Try again," she says. "Practice makes perfect." Uh-huh. I try again and start to get it. Sort of. Head under, blow bubbles. Head above, take a breath. "Ok, good!" says mom. "Now let's have you lay in my arms again, and do what you've been doing with your head. Don't worry about your arms and legs. Hesitant, I lay in her arms and do the bubble and breath thing. Then I take a break. "Good, dear, you're getting it," she says. "You rest, and watch me."

She pushes herself off and does the crawl. She is a veritable torpedo in the water, a strong composed swimming machine. Mom is small and powerful. She swims like she could go across the lake. Her torso rotates in syncopation with her arm strokes and her head, her kicking feet hardly make a splash above water. She turns and comes back. I stand there watching her, amazed. Mom will prove time and time again, she is full of surprises. She pops up from the water and pushes her hair back over her head and despite the fact she smokes like a blast furnace is not even remotely winded and smiles. I look at her, my expression betrays my awe. "Want to try laying in my arms again?" she asks.

"O.K.," I say. I think maybe I can do this. But what we are both about to find out is mom is coordinated. And I am not. This it turns out, is a basic component of my nature. "He can't walk and chew gum at the same time," comes to mind. And for most people it's a funny little quip, but for me, it's true. When chewing Bazooka Bubble Gum was popular, I got in on the action, but had to sit in a chair. My buddies would be ready to go run in the woods while chewing their gum and I'd take mine out of my mouth before taking off. They'd look at me like, "you weirdo, that gum hasn't lost its flavor yet." And I'd look at them like, "you wouldn't understand."

"This time kick your feet at the same time," she says. I do this, but more flail than kick. I breathe in another mouthful of water and start choking and jump out of mom's arms. She can see I've had enough. "Let's call it quits for today," she says, and this is more than okey-dokey with me. I dog paddle and goof around to my heart's content.

After many more attempts, it will become apparent this stroke is completely beyond me. I will flail, thrash, sink, inhale great quantities of water, choke and get frustrated, but I will not do the crawl. As it turns out, the side stroke becomes my swim of choice and I will become a strong swimmer, and swim for miles if I like. But forget the crawl. Watching people do it just amazes me. Being separated from everyone else by vast sweeps of ocean, lots of strange things have happened in Australia, and one of them is Australians have evolved super-human coordination.

We're all tired and cold and one of us is cranky and we'd all like to get back into the boat and go back to camp. This is when we realize a ladder would be very handy. When you're in open water, there is no graceful way to get in a boat without a ladder. Mom gives Vic and me boosts, Vic first. Vic is more coordinated than me, but she's slippery as a seal and having never done this before, well, it's an experiment. She slithers and grabs and heaves her way and gets aboard. Now it's my turn. Froggy is what you might call me, I'm slippery and squiggly and mom boosts me and arms and legs go in all directions except into the boat and Vic leans in my direction to help and the boat tips waaay over. Waves slop over the gunnel, which adds a sense of alarm that we're going to tip the thing over. In my struggles I'm doing my best not to kick my mother in the jaw and somehow eventually manage to get one foot hooked over the gunnel and flop into the dirty bilge of the boat. Laying there in a tangled heap, I am covered with sandy fish slime bilge slop.

Now it's mom's turn, and she has no one to give her a boost. Being 5'1" is in these circumstances a distinct disadvantage, but she is a person not easily daunted. "When I get up on the gunnel, you two move to the other side of the boat," she says. "Three of us on one side, we would tip it over." Mom grasps the gunnel and jumps up, putting her weight on her hands. But with the boat tipping toward her, her feet go underneath the hull. Vic and I want to help her, but she says, "you stay on the other side…" and we comply, sitting there expecting anything could happen and feeling helpless. Mom tips her torso into the boat. Oh, and did I mention she has big boobs? Well, it looks like her boobs might come flying out of her low cut bathing suit at any moment and this strikes me as pretty funny and I snicker. Both mom and Vic shoot me looks, like, "Buster, it's NOT FUNNY." So I make a gallant effort to mind my manners and not look just in case they do pop out, but I'm also concerned mom might need help so I kind of have to look.

Mom slithers and grunts and gets one foot up over the gunnel and she's headed for the bilge and her butt is sticking up in the air and she starts laughing and if dad were here he'd take a picture. I want to tickle her but manage not to. Good thing. And finally she's in the boat, laying there, laughing her head off and we all laugh, three clowns sitting in a boat. The next time we go into Wolfeboro we go to Winnipesaukee Motor Craft, not to buy a boat, but to buy a boat ladder. While mom picks out a ladder, I look at the boats. There's a little ember of fascination taking light in me for boats.

. . .

The 4th of July is a big deal in Wolfeboro. Come to think of it, most declarations of independence, signed or otherwise are big deals. Seemingly, all of New England swarms to Wolfeboro. Traffic gets backed up for miles from the blinking light. Traffic around the entire perimeter of Lake Winnipesaukee gets backed up, roadways turn into big snarls of cars, parking lots, essentially. People are hot and sweaty and just want to get to wherever they're going which is close to the water and take a swim and eat hot dogs and hamburgers cooked on the grill and watch girls in bathing suits. Some of us, that is. We vow as a family: do not go anywhere near town on the 4th of July. No exceptions. Not one. Well, maybe dad sneaks in for beer, I don't know. There is *one* agreed upon exception - the town fair and firework display. This is a rite of summer.

So as traffic snarls and tempers flare, we live the good life at Robie's. The campground, like everywhere else, is packed and full of festive energy. The septic system for the bath house however - remember, back woods engineering - can't handle the crowd and is also packed full. When the guy with the pump truck arrives and hops down from the cab, he's not looking so festive, but he does look like he's making money. It's sunny and hot and he stands there in the hot and the stink and empties the septic tank. Little does he know, he'll be back before the end of the weekend.

It's always sunny and hot on the 4th, unless of course it's rainy and cold. We go swimming at the sandbar and feel pretty smart with our new boat ladder and we run around in the woods and relish the smells of all the cookouts. We light firecrackers and throw them at each other and run and scream. Someone always brings some cherry bombs or better yet, some M-80's and when one of those babies goes off everyone jumps and hoots. KaBOOM! I snuck a cherry bomb under the lawn chair Pamp was sitting in once. When it went off everyone scattered, hit the decks... except Pamp. He sat there, didn't even flinch.

Midday dad fires up the hibachi. He carefully packs it with charcoal briquettes and soaks it with lighter fluid. Literally. He soaks it until it's dripping and then throws a match at it. He's learned to not set up the hibachi under any tree cover. We didn't have to call the fire department that time, but for a while it was touch and go. So he does this out in the open, preferably with sand underneath. And vaVOOM! The hibachi bursts into flames and he stands back with a look of supreme satisfaction on his face. Me. Man. Fire builder. He looks at us and grins and purposely sticks his belly out for effect. Fatty tidbits sticking to the grills from our last cookout vaporize instantly. The air above the hibachi is all wavey. Looking at dad through it, he's all wiggly like in a funhouse. In a manner of speaking, this is a funhouse.

We have hot dogs and hamburgers and all the accouterments, and macaroni salad and potato salad and Kool-Aid, and intoxicants for the grown-ups. Barb brings a pot of her chili and an aspic salad, and except for the aspic salad, life is good. Vic and I force down small quantities of it because Barb is a sweetheart and we know she loves us and we love her. Plus, she always asks if we've had some and it's nice to say yes and not be lying. Even after all the samples of aspic salad over all the years, Vic and I still hate the stuff. It's made from horse hooves, after all, and think of where *they've* been.

We eat massive quantities of everything else. This is the life of running and swimming and fresh air. If you took all the food we eat in a summer and stacked it up, it'd be quite a pile. We do however save room for strawberry shortcake. This is the real deal. Barb makes the shortcakes and we heap on the strawberries and the freshly whipped cream. We've been swimming and goofing around and had a cookout, and to top it all off we're eating strawberry shortcake, sitting under the pines with a breeze coming off the lake … It's the 4th of July. This is living.

The fireworks won't start until dark, which in these northern climes comes late. But now that we've at least partially recovered from the cookout, we cram into the Peugeot and head for town. "The Peug," as we affectionately call it is a fun little car, and like everything French, it marches to the beat of a different drummer. For instance, none of the levers and switches on the dashboard are labeled. You are supposed to know what they do, and if you don't and you think it'd be nice to turn on the radio, you might get the defroster. Or the windshield wipers. The Peug is equipped with a 4-cylinder engine, which at this time in The United States of America, the land of the free and home of the V8, is otherwise almost unheard of. It has a sunroof, again, unheard of, and the interior smells like leather and hot dust. Oh, and later models, and I promise I'll stop talking about Peugeot's after this detail: they sprayed them with a coat of rubber before the paint, thinking this would prevent stone chips. *Viva la France!* But it didn't work very well. In time, giant patches of paint were routinely seen flying off the cars as they hummed down the road. Amazing, Peugeot is still in business.

Peculiarities aside or perhaps because of them, we love the Peug. It gets us to Wolfeboro and we park in our secret place near the old power house. The closer we get to the fair, the greater the throng of people, the energy of the crowd condenses and swells in waves. Moms and dads holding their kids hand's, shouting, everyone is excited, streaming to the source of light and music and commotion. Mom brings the plaid wool car blanket. The grass on the field we'll be viewing the fireworks from will be damp, so it will be nice to sit on.

The fair is a village in itself. Food and trinket vendors have their trailers painted white with bold red lettering describing their wares, and are all lit up with white and yellow fluorescent tubes. Generators thrum in the background. People carry around smoked turkey legs which can also be used to club an adversary, if required. Stuffed animals, strings of bright plastic beads, but where's the cotton candy? This is what I'm most interested in. There are games of chance and rides. Except for the teacups we stay away from the rides. Getting dizzy is fun, but throwing up is not. Vic and I are drawn to the teacups. We have been known to ride them over and over again, long after the rest of our party has moved on, we're still going 'round and 'round hooting and screaming. And lo, there they are. "Mom, dad!" I yell.

I grab Vic's hand. "We're gonna ride the teacups!" And I haul Vic away, and when she sees them, she's running ahead of me. We get in line which for some reason is always short. People don't know what they're missing... they'd rather wait for a half hour to ride the gut-wrenching *Octopus* or *The Whip!* We check that we have enough money and we're off.

The wiry little guy taking the money looks like trouble. His eyes dart around, he gives everyone a going over, giving special attention to the girls and grins and sucks his teeth. A burning cigarette dangles from his lips and the pack is rolled into his shirt sleeve. He wears a filthy painters apron slung low around his waist to put money in and make change. If he gives Vic one ounce of trouble I'll smack him, and fortunately he doesn't because even though he's a small guy he's still about twice my size. Once we're seated in our teacup and the platter starts going around, this is all that matters. We zoom around and reverse direction without warning, we strain against the centrifugal force and have the time of our lives. All too soon it comes to an end and we get off, all topsy-turvy and Vic says, "Let's do it again!" And I'm with her. We ride the teacups one more time and are about to go a third round when dad steps in.

"How about a game of ring-toss?" he asks, not realizing this is about as exciting as a game of pick up sticks. Then again, he is a grown-up.

"But dad..." I whine. "Can't we do the teacups one more time?"

He looks at me, raising his eyebrows. Few people understand the thrill of the teacups as Vic and me. "Or maybe some cotton candy?" He suggests. "I know where they're set up." With this he has unleashed the secret weapon. All else fades into oblivion. Cast under his spell, we happily tag along.

Sugar, salt and fat. Over the past million or so years, the desire for these three food groups has slowly but surely been hard-wired into us, and when you look around at carnival food that's all you see. And cotton candy, yeah baby, is #1 on the list. There is one other key ingredient - a splash of Red Dye #40. Darned if I know how the machine that spins the stuff actually works, but it's a lot of fun to watch. I think they start out with a left over jet engine from a fighter plane, they stuff it with sugar and dye, put it in reverse and hit the starter button. It's a miracle, and one of the greatest contributions of all time to childhood happiness and the dentistry business. There's a long line and the wait is forever, but in this case forever is worth it. Longingly we watch kids walking away with their cotton candy.

The trailer is brilliantly lit, the fragrance of hot sugar wafts about. As much as cotton candy does for the happiness of children, it appears to do nothing for the people making it. There are two polished jet engines in operation, and large sacks of sugar are piled up beside a 55-gallon drum of the red dye in the back. Everyone in the trailer looks hot, sweaty and bored out of their minds. And they're all coated with wisps of pink sugar. At last it's my turn. I look up at the woman about to make my cotton candy and smile, she looks at me for a second, the slightest bit of a smile flickers across her face. But she concentrates on the task, slowly spinning the paper cone around and around and I watch with amazement as the delicate pink strands accumulate. She is a cotton candy *Artiste*. I hope she gives mine an extra twirl. When she finishes and hands it to me, it looks plenty big enough, and I am thrilled. It's puffy and hot and most importantly, sweet. Wickedly sweet. Sugar is king! Vic gets hers and I scrutinize it, and O.K., it looks just about the same size as mine.

The fairgrounds are located on a hill overlooking on Wolfeboro Bay, we can just make out the town docks, and Lake

Winnipesaukee stretches out and beyond for miles. There's also the park with a gazebo on the shore, it's quintessential New England, all about as scenic as it gets. Mom has already staked our claim on the field for watching the fireworks, which will be launched over the water. It's getting toward dark so we head in this direction, like a lot of other people, to settle in for the show. Turns out it's already so dark we have a hard time finding mom. Dad takes our hands, which by now are gloved in a pink, sticky sugar coating, and leads us around. We do our best not to trip over people. Falling, cotton candy first, in the dark, into a family gathered on their blanket would not be good. After searching high and low we locate mom, she has a primo spot and we sit down on the scratchy wool blanket. Dew is falling out of the sky and it's getting chilly. We huddle together. Those spots of shared body heat feel good.

People come from around the lake in their boats, and anchor in the bay to watch the show. All we see are their twinkling red and green and white navigation lights and there are lots of them. It's quite a scene, reflections streak across the water. There might be some drinking going on out there, which makes it a heck of a good night to have a collision. I can almost hear the crunches and scrapes and swearing.

And then, VaVoom! Off goes the first rocket leaving a brilliant white trail and BANG!, a spray of red sparklers... and BANG!, white ones, and BANG! there's blue, and the boaters blow their horns and the crowd cheers. The booms are scary but it is a spectacle, we watch and ooo... and ahhh... and whistle.

And on goes the display, great percussive shots into the air, rainbows of brilliant colors, pops and bangs, followed by the cacophony of horns from the boats. I watch faint silhouettes of the people on the water's edge who are lighting the fireworks. Points of red light from the flares they use flutter about. It's the dance of mysterious fire shamans. This is a job I'd like to have, lighting off the fireworks. I bet it's more fun than a barrel of monkeys. The grand finale is almost more than I can stand, I'm shaking with adrenaline and sugar and cold. I hide my head under a corner of the blanket but after every boom I peek up to watch... and ooo... and ahhh...

Because it would be unpatriotic of Mother Nature to rain on the 4th of July, she holds off until just after, and then lets go. Not to waste any time about it, starting on the 5th, or if we've been good, the 6th, it starts raining, and keeps raining for a solid week. Out come the board games from the trunk of the Buick and we make a trip to McDuffee's.

In the tent, everything has gone beyond damp to soggy, even Tippy. The poor cat looks like a scrawny wrung out mop. He goes out only to do his business and comes back, soaked, and with feet caked with dirt and pine needles. "I want to go home," he meows, and seeing how we don't understand cat very well, we rub him down with a towel which is only marginally less soggy than he is. "Next best thing to going home, I suppose," he meows, and hops up on Vic's pillow and one by one shakes his feet and licks the dirt from between his toes. How he does this without impaling his tongue on his extended claws is a mystery. He then curls up and takes a nap. Tonight when it's time to go to bed, Vic's going to have a little surprise, her pillow covered with soggy cat dirt.

"How about we go to Bailey's for lunch, and then a trip to McDuffee's?" asks mom. I immediately think of a fried clam boat and a Coke and am all for it. Somehow all I think about is the food, McDuffee's is off in mist somewhere. Vic is not so excited, but seeing how the pages of her new issue of *Tiger Beat* are mostly stuck together, she's game. "Get on your slickers and let's go," says mom. She is definitely up for getting out of the tent. "Tippunze, you're on your own for a bit," she says.

Tippy looks up, glares at mom and gives her a silent meow, "Can't you see I was napping?" But all is quickly forgiven and he tucks his nose in under his foreleg and goes back to dreaming about deep sea tuna fishing off Baja.

Bailey's is a madhouse. That's on a clear day. But today it's a mad madhouse when everyone has discovered they'd like to check in voluntarily, especially the moms. We wait for a table. The front foyer is packed with people ahead of us so we wait outside under the awning. Rain pours off the edge of the blue and white striped awning, a miniature lake is forming in the parking lot. Grown-ups walk around it, kids through it. We're encouraged when happily fed customers leave and the line inches forward. I hope they don't run out of clams before we get a table, that would spoil my day. We get seated in a booth in the original part of the building. The walls, the tables, the seats are all made of knotty pine, finished in many coats of amber varnish. The windows are louvered strips of glass, today they're closed, and all fogged up. The seats have no cushions - they don't want folks getting too comfortable - and sitting on the varnished wood, in shorts, is fine until you decide to move. This is when you discover the backs of your tender sunburned thighs are stuck to the finish and won't budge. The nubile college age waitress comes by and takes our order, they still have clams! Any movement is going to hurt, but on the pretense of needing to use the boys room I get up to run around. It feels like I'm leaving a layer of skin behind. We often go to Bailey's when it's raining, so it's a plus we have no memory for pain.

By the time I get back our drinks have arrived, glasses of water, Cokes for Vic and me and mom's having coffee. Caffeine, oh blessed caffeine. Sweat pours off the sides of the icy glasses
110

and puddles on the table. When you pick up your glass and tip it to your mouth, drops of cold water fall into your lap, making it look like you've peed in your pants. Vic and I make wiggly worms with the wrappers from our straws. Wiggly worms are a hoot.

The waitress arrives with our plates stacked up one arm. She looks like she's just about to go around the twist. Completely, utterly frazzled. But she has our orders right. Mom gets her lobster roll, Vic gets her BLT and I get my clam boat, we're all happy. Why they call it a clam *boat* when you don't use a boat to get clams is beyond me. Maybe it's the red plastic basket it comes in, which sort of looks like a boat. Not any boat I'd be caught in, but anyway… it's heaped with fried clams, battered and crispy and glistening with hot saturated fats with a generous helping of crinkle cut French fries, crispy on the outside and poofy steaming potato on the inside. The man at the Fryolator is a genius. Nestled in my boat are white paper cups, one filled with ketchup, the other with homemade tartar sauce made with dill pickles. Suddenly our table goes quiet as we dive in. Oh, deep-fried heaven.

The waitress comes back, of course we'll have refills on our Cokes and coffee! And by the time she comes back with the refills, we've licked our plates (I've licked my boat) clean. Dessert? Of course we'll have dessert. Mom orders her standard hot fudge sundae and Vic and I each are about to order banana splits when mom steps in. The banana splits are huge, you get the banana, three scoops of ice cream, a mountain of whip cream, chocolate sauce, strawberry sauce, chopped nuts, maraschino cherries complete with stems; banana splits are the bomb! "I think you two can *split* a banana split," she says in that special tone that's friendly but means business and we know it. So we don't give her any lip, and instead look at each other like this is awful but we'll put up with it and bicker about what flavor the middle scoop of ice cream will be until the waitress is about to cry and mom says, "make the middle scoop peppermint stick," and the waitress disappears.

"Mom! I hate peppermint stick!" says Vic. And I sit there and coyly stick my tongue out at her because I love peppermint stick and she knows it. She glowers at me and sneers, "you wait, you are so going to get it." With this, I know the ride to McDuffee's is going to be fun. By the time we leave, the table resembles something between a landfill and a war zone. Bits of fried things, spilled Coke, dead wiggly worms in pools of water litter the table-scape. Soggy lipstick and coffee stained napkins. Busboys are the unsung heroes of the food service industry.

We run to the car and jump in. The windows are opaque with fog. We're already on our way out of the lot when mom says, "I'm going to turn on the air…" and I'm about to mouth "I'm going to turn on the air…" to her back when Vic leans over and gives the side of my thigh a really bad monkey bite and whispers, "peppermint stick." I scream out in pain and mom stomps on the brakes and turns around. Her expression is scary wild. Maybe that third cup of coffee was not such a good idea.

"Now if you two are going to fight!…" and we can see a flicker of indecision cross her face, "…we'll go back to Robie's right now." None of us, especially mom, wants to go back to Robie's, so Vic and I move to opposite corners and promise to be complete little angels and a trip to McDuffee's would be a whole lotta fun, and we'll be good, won't we Vic? The driver behind us is getting impatient and blows his horn. Mom snaps around, looks both ways, sees long lines of oncoming traffic bearing down on us from all directions and floors it. The old Buick leaps to attention and we roar off to Ossipee, trailing a cloud of mist and unburned leaded super.

McDuffee's is in the old Grange Hall on Pork Hill Road in Ossipee. Years ago, someone in the area must have kept pigs, one would think, on the hill, down that road. Mr. and Mrs. McDuffee used to operate a general store, but they've drifted into selling "antiques," and lots of other stuff, mostly in the genre of what is commonly referred to as junk. Lots of junk. But because it's old junk, it is fascinating junk.

Vic is apparently satisfied with the monkey bite she got in, so we manage to get to McDuffee's without further conflict. The rain is coming down in buckets. The Grange Hall building is a clapboarded three story structure with a steep pitched roof and a porch on the front facing the road. The stark building stands as a sentinel to another time, and is straight and true, a testament to being very well built. We leap out of the car and run for the porch. Sheets of water pour off the eaves and falls on the dirt yard, creating a line of glistening pebbles. On the porch we shake most of the water off our coats and then go inside.

A small bell on the door tinkles when we open it, and over the foot-worn threshold we step into another world. Except for the ticking of a clock and the occasional snap from the fire in the pot bellied stove, it is quiet and still. The McDuffee's are true country folk, smart in country ways, kindly, and very reserved. Mrs. McDuffee sits behind a glass top counter and looks up from whatever she's fiddling with. "Good aftahnoon," she says, clipping her words with a prim smile, and this is all she says. She is heavily built, has her fine silver hair pulled back in a tight wound bun and wears a cotton house coat with small floral print, and a cardigan sweater. A number of the buttons are missing from the sweater. We say hello and wander around. Stacks of old books. Trays of flatware, and if you look closely some of it's sterling. Buckets of kitchen utensils. Cases of jewelry, pocket watches, daguerreotypes of long forgotten farm folk, trinkets. Hair pins, combs, pocket knives, parts of horse harnesses, brass Model T hub caps. Head lights. Button hooks, carpenter's tools. Pots and pans, cast iron, white enamel with blue or red trim. Popover pans. Bed pans. Pitchers and wash basins. Glass insulators. Bear traps. Oil lamps and farrier's tools. Ammunition belts.

It's easy to spend hours here. So many of these things in their silent ways, tell the old stories. The door bell tinkles, it's Mr. McDuffee coming in. He's a giant square backed man. He wears a red and black plaid wool jacket, green work pants heavily stained with oil and grime, work boots and a green billed cap, as soiled as his pants. He's carrying an armload of firewood and methodically places the sticks in the wood box next to the stove. Mr. McDuffee smiles when he sees us but is silent. When I find some unknown artifact I take it to one of them and ask, "what's this?" and in their kindly way I get a word in answer, maybe two. We always leave McDuffee's with a prize, sometimes a bag full. I still have a spatula I got there. The blade is extremely thin spring steel and it has a wood handle with the last remants of green paint. I've turned a lot of eggs with it.

When we get back to the tent, dad's there. He took off from work early. We show him our prizes, asking him if he knows what they are, and he always does. Amazing the things he knows. He looks over my goodies, considers them carefully and picking up one artifact for closer examination, says, "that's an anvil stake." He looks at me with raised eyebrows and smiles. I don't know how he does it.

He's brought homemade pea soup from the freezer at home and we'll have it for dinner. Rain continues to fall and it's cold. We huddle in the tent, it smells of wet canvas, acrid and oily, but we're snug. Mom makes cornbread in a cast iron skillet, which she bought on one of our trips to McDuffee's, and heats the soup. Pea soup is something we love, but it makes us, well,

114

especially dad, a little bit gassy if you know what I mean. Tonight we will refer to our sleeping bags as "fart sacks," and giggle and hoot. Poor mom, having to sleep in the same end of the tent with dad. There surely will be some explosions in the night followed by some comments.

We have a card table set up in the middle room with a jigsaw puzzle laid out on it. We've been working at it since it started raining three days ago. We have dinner at the table, on top of the puzzle taking extra care not to spill soup or crumbs. After dinner we get back to the puzzle. Mom likes to get puzzles that are reproductions of famous paintings, Van Gogh's Sunflowers, Monet's Chartres Cathedral, this one is Leutze's Washington Crossing the Delaware. Dad is especially fond of this picture. It's Christmas night and it looks really cold and there he is, General Washington standing up in the lead boat, with a bunch of other guys. The boat sits perilously low in the water. A couple of the guys push chunks of ice out of the way. Man, they look cold. In another boat, men do their best to control horses, imagine horses getting antsy in a leaky old boat! The white one must be Washington's.

Between the stove and lantern, it's toasty in the tent. Looking at the puzzle I feel pretty lucky. I wouldn't want to be out there on the Delaware. Dad farts. He acts like nothing has happened, no grin or anything, he just keeps concentrating on the puzzle. Mom shakes her head, she knows this is only the beginning. I snicker. Vic says, "Dad, that's gross." Tippy looks up from his Calo and retreats to the furthest corner of the tent and sits like a jellybean and glowers at dad. When a cat thinks something smells worse than Calo, you know it's bad. Then dad cuts another one.

"Bunk!" says mom. "Must you?"

"What?" asks dad, still as though nothing has happened. "Has anyone seen the end of George's scabbard?" he asks.

"You may act innocent," says mom. "But we know better - you stink!" Vic, mom and I nod our heads.

Dad casts mom a sideways glance, "She who lives in glass house should not throw stones," he says. And things only go downhill from here.

Toward bed time, dad fills the tank of the Coleman heater. It's cold and damp and once we put out the lantern, it will get just too cold in the tent. Vic and I get our tooth brushes and tooth paste and go to the bath house. We each have flashlights. Barb and Pamp have the windows of the cottage closed, warm lights glow from inside. I can see Barb sitting in the front room rocker, it looks like she's mending something. After all the rain, and now with the cold, the bug zappers and suckers are quiet. It's stopped raining for the moment, there are a few openings in the clouds and we can see stars. A breeze comes up and giant drops of water fall from the pines. When one of these drops smacks you it's like getting hit with a pebble. Splat! Walking back to the tent, it's all glowing blue from the lantern and we can see mom's shadow moving around. The breeze picks up, bringing down more of the big drops. Splat! Splat! We can hear waves lapping the dark shore.

We come around to the front of the tent, and find dad lighting the Coleman heater. A tower of flames jumps up from it, which in a moment will settle down. Tellingly, they don't make these contraptions anymore. How many tents, how many families, how many acres of forest went up in flames from these things, I wonder. But once it calms down and glows orange red it does put out the heat. My sleeping bag is cold and damp, and I shiver when I first get into it. In a moment I start to warm. Vic's snug in her bag and mom and dad wish us, "Sleep tight, don't let the bedbugs bite." Mom leaves the curtains open so the heat will circulate. She and dad talk in hushed tones. Tippy sneaks inside Vic's bag and curls up with her. My monkey bite still hurts, but I love Vic. And one could argue I had it coming to me. It's been a great day, and knowing you are loved is the greatest feeling in life. I fall fast, fast asleep.

.   .   .

The school year is a time of confinement, boredom and trouble. An analogy has been made between the public school and the prison systems. We use them to get populations we are afraid of off the streets and control them with the smallest and lowest paid staffs possible. To whatever extent this may be true, there is no question when I am in school, I feel like a prisoner. And not surprisingly, like a prisoner, I act out.

I am the kid who pilfers strips of magnesium tape from the science lab - why they have this stuff around I could never figure out - and going home on the bus, ignites and waves them out the window burning with a brilliant white hot flame, much to the consternation of the bus driver and other motorists. I get kicked off the bus, which turns out to be a good thing. After a day's confinement, I need the walk.

I am the kid who stands up in the middle of the social studies teacher's presentation and says, "That's stupid!" and promptly gets kicked out of class.

I am the kid who on a cold fall day, after the teacher finally gets the class settled down, will say, "Look! it's snowing out!" Of course it isn't but the entire class, including the teacher, will jerk their heads to look out the window and the hard won calm is completely broken. It is especially funny that in a given class period, I can get them to look out the window two or three more times this way.

I am the kid who will stand up in front of French class and recite conversations with my fellow wise guy partner Russell, very... ploddingly... slowly, and the class will laugh and the kindly teacher will stop us. "Boys, speak faster," she says. With this, we fly, we rattle off the words at the speed of light and the class erupts into hysterics. The teacher stops us. "No, boys, that's too fast. Try speaking more slowly," she says with the patience of a saint. We go back to glacial. We get sent to stand in the hallway a few times for this. But it is a heck of a lot of fun.

In other situations I just give up. In math class I get stuck on the concept of zero. After all, if 1 indicates the presence of the apple and -1 indicates the absence of the apple, then why do we have this weird 0 thing in between? Would somebody please tell me? You either have the apple or not. The longer I ponder this, the further behind I get. By the time I stop pondering zero, the teacher and her all-controlling syllabus have marched on to who knows what, trigonometry probably and I am completely, utterly lost. Oh well, failing math isn't such a big deal. Einstein did.

In English Literature, we are required to read the *Iliad*. Only 602 pages. O.K., as an adult I've read a lot of books and some of those have been the big fat ones, the ones translated from Russian and Greek. But the *Iliad*? The few times I've considered it, browsing in the bookstore, I read, or rather, attempt to read a page or two and my eyes immediately roll back in my head and I get dizzy. So, I sleep through English Literature class. Mine is not the only snore from around the room.

The icy grey skies and snowfall of winter give way to wet grey skies and the slush and mud of spring. Everyone in our family, each in our own way, starts anticipating going to the lake. My way is paying even less attention in school. One dismally overcast Saturday morning dad says to me, "After lunch let's go to Haggett's… something there I want to show you. Then we'll go to Chez Louis'."

I practically pounce on dad. "Do you mean Haggett's *Marine?*"

"That'd be the one," he says.

I sling a barrage of questions at dad. "Why are we going to Haggett's? What's at Haggett's?"

All he will say is, "You'll see." This is when the man of few words' behavior is put to best use. Gosh, I wish he'd give me a clue, but no way. Dad however, does smile, and this is pure guy stuff which is the best.

I can barely contain myself and mom makes toasted cheese sandwiches with rat cheese and Grey Poupon mustard and homemade bread and butter pickles on the side and I eat quickly and am itching to go. Positively itching. When dad finishes, I drag him out the door. We get in the Peug and head for Haggett's. The word marine means one thing and we already have a boat ladder.

With a few summers on the lake now under my belt, boats have found their way onto my radar screen. Boats mean access to the open water and open up whole new worlds of possibility. I've observed all sorts of them on the lake, they can be scary and fast, calm and slow. They are fascinating, not to mention cool and fun. We get to Haggett's, a low slung, rambling building in the pines. Boats of all description sit around the yard, there's a rack of canoes under the shed, and inside is the ship's store. Coils of rope, anchors, fire extinguishers, bronze cleats and chocks and nuts and bolts, compasses, navigation lights, bright orange life preservers, water skis lined up leaning against the wall. Fuel tanks and hoses, bumpers, engines, and trolling motors. Out back is the service area. We can hear engines running, revving up, getting tune-ups, some sputter and wallow. Mechanics listen to them and with screwdrivers and wrenches, perform their brand of surgery. It's a feast for the senses and so exciting, all toward breaking the bonds of land and feeling the freedom of being on the water.

Dana Haggett sees us coming and smiles and says hello, he's a sturdy guy with close cropped hair and glasses hanging on the end of his nose. He looks at me over his glasses and says, "Now let's see. I think we have something here for you." He riffles through a pile of paperwork, and I am about to explode. He pulls out a yellow carbon copy, studies it and says, "C'mon outside to the yard." He leads us outside and through a gate in a chain link fence. Boats are all over the place, and there, sitting up on blocks is the Starcraft. Dana puts his hand on the gunnel. "What do you think of this one?" he asks.

I look at dad, he's looking at me and he says, "This is our boat. You think it'll do?"

I am bowled over. I touch the boat, look at it, and barely above a whisper say, "Wow... yeah. It's a great boat." Dana and dad watch as I walk around it. It's an aluminum 12 footer, white on the outside, light green on the inside with three varnished mahogany bench seats. And it has a sky blue 6 horsepower Evinrude engine on the back. Six h.p.! Twice that of Harvey's boat! This boat's gonna fly! When I come around to dad and Dana

I stop, ogle over the boat some more. It's amazing. I look at dad again. "Thanks," I say. He looks like he's about to cry.

He puts his hand on my head and gives it a scruff. "You're welcome. There's miles of smiles in this boat," he says. Dad and I shake Dana's hand. Dad's taught me you give a man a good grip when you shake his hand. No dead fish. This is another small step into manhood. And so with the deal set and agreed upon, dad and I head for Louis'. Dad and I will get a roof rack at Sears next weekend to bring the boat home.

"Chez Louis'," is dad's name for Louis' Diner. Like Haggett's, it's on the Heights. And it's near the airport where dad works, so he knows Louis' and a lot of the clientele. We go there every once in a while for coffee and doughnuts, the building is a genuine old diner with polished stainless steel cladding and a lunch counter and booths inside. We sit at the counter on the rotating stools, dad orders coffee with milk for me which is actually milk with some coffee . I love going to Louis' with dad.

This time, to celebrate, instead of doughnuts we have pie with our coffee. Even though it's well after lunch time, the place is busy. On this grey afternoon, quite a few people apparently are thinking coffee and pie. I have cherry pie, my favorite. It has a lattice crust on top and so, O.K., the filling is mostly corn starch goo, but it has a few cherries in it, and it tastes like cherries. This is a diner, not the Ritz Carlton.

"Now I want it to be clear, the Starcraft is our family's boat," says dad. "Your mother and I want you to use it and have fun with it, but it's for all of us. Do you understand?"

"Yes, dad," I say. This is a serious conversation. "Can I go out in it by myself?" I ask, eagerly.

"Let's see how you do handling it," he says. Dad sips his coffee and sets down the mug. The waitress comes by with a fresh pot. She's moving fast and the coffee sloshes around, right up to the brim of the glass globe but never over. She fills our cups without asking. Dad nods and she dashes off. "We'll take it one step at a time," he says in the voice of reason.

Layering caffeine and sugar on top of excitement, I rotate back and forth on my stool, envisioning great journeys in the boat, epic tales of high seas adventure. "It's so cool," I say. "Thanks, dad." Many of the adventures I dream about will come to pass, as will quite a few others I have no way of knowing about.

"You're welcome," he says. Dad nods his head and finishes his pie.

Midweek dad gets a roof rack kit from Sears, and the coming Saturday morning, after studying too many pages of bewildering instructions, we tackle the job of installing it on the Peug. The rack is a shining example of tremendous optimism and poor design. We set the two box section steel tubes across the roof of the car on towels so not to scratch the paint, and from there, it is complete confusion. Nuts, bolts, little plastic pieces, brackets and thing-a-ma-bobs. "Attach supports loosely to box sections with bolts lock washers and nuts provided. Attach plastic u-channels to supports, set in rain gutter. Tighten bolts A - H, insert plastic plugs into ends of box sections..."

Tippy comes out, hops on the hood of the car, then up onto the roof and sits down on the edge of one of the towels. And this is where he stays, to supervise, until we are finished. He eventually gets bored and takes a nap in the middle of it all. Four hours of fiddling and pushing and pulling and tapping and tightening later, famished, we step back and admire our work.

Dad looks at me. "Well, Orville, think it'll fly?" he asks.

"Wilbur, I guess we'll find out," I say. With this, we go inside and see what's for lunch. In my excitement to get to Haggett's I inhale a hot pastrami on onion roll sandwich and a glass of milk. Then I sit there and suffer as dad advances on his like a tectonic plate. Maybe my perspective is a bit skewed but finally, after an interminable five minutes we're on our way.

Before we get to the end of the street, we discover Sears skipped the wind tunnel test on the roof rack. It whistles. It howls. It hums and buzzes and moans, depending on how fast we go and the direction and speed of prevailing winds. We look at one another with furrowed brows. "Getting to Wolfeboro ought to be fun," says dad, but in a Quixotic way, the racket adds to the amusement. When we get to Haggett's, Dana's glad to see us. Our ears are ringing and heads buzzing and we have to ask him to speak up. Dad's brought some tools, and we check the security of the roof rack before loading the boat. Always thinkin', and it's secure enough. We hope. Dana enlists the help of a few guys from the shop to lift the boat onto the rack. They make it look easy. Then they put the engine and fuel tank in the trunk.

Part of the grand design of the roof rack are four giant "J" bolts to hold the boat down. Imagine an upside down letter "J." Dinky plastic caps are provided to cover the tip of the hook. The hook is to go over the gunnel of the boat and the threaded stem goes through a hole in the roof rack. A washer and wing-nut are tightened up from below, thus clamping the gunnel of the boat to the rack. According to said grand design. Looks like it'll work, and it does. Sort of. But wing nuts? Tightened with your fingers is supposed to be tight enough? Dad brought pliers and he tightens the things to within an inch of their lives. If plastic tipped "J" bolts with flat washers and wing nuts have lives.

We grab ahold of the gunnels and tug the boat this way and that. It's fairly secure. Well, ok, it slides around a little bit.

Dana eyes the whole shebang with suspicion, goes into the shop and reappears with a spool of rope. "Let's tie it off, stem and stern," he says, and without waiting for a response gets to work. Unlike just about everyone else in the known universe, Dana knows how to tie knots. The actual correct knots. He ties bowlines and rigger's knots and with a flash of his pocket knife cuts off the excess line and before we know it, the boat is... *more* secure.

"We're only going across town," says dad (famous last words), and everyone seems happy enough. We go inside, and while I'm eyeing the impressive nautical gear, dad pays Dana and gets a bill of sale with serial numbers and things written on it and we all shake hands again. Dad and I get in the Peug and look at each other and grin.

"Can we open the sun roof?" I ask.

"Don't see why not," says dad, and he reaches up to the little crank handle in the roof and cranks and cranks until he works up a sweat and like the curtain on a stage it builds anticipation, slowly opening, revealing a view of the inside of the boat. Cool. Sit in a car, look up, and see a boat.

Embarking on the saga of nautical discovery, the next little detail we get slapped in the face with has to do with the center of gravity. Adding a hundred and fifty pounds to the top of a little car, makes it go up. Way up. This is glaringly apparent in the first corner we navigate and the car tips way, way over.

Whoaa! Make note in ship's log: Take corners slowly with boat on top of car. At least the thing doesn't come flying off. On the likelihood of this happening, there is still some question.

Safely at home, we are faced with getting the boat off the top of the car. Hoisting and moving a hundred and fifty pounds of unwieldy boat over your head when you don't have a bunch of guys around turns out to be a project. We could call Mr. G., but he's short and the G.'s are out of town for the weekend. Mom comes out to survey the scene. Too bad, she's shorter than Mr. G. As we think of it, too bad Mrs. G. isn't around. She's as tall as dad, and probably stronger.

We fiddle around with undoing the J bolts and rope, taking care not to misplace all the bits and pieces. Dad stands back and surveys the scene. "First, use brute force. If that fails, get a bigger hammer," says he, with his mischievous grin, then adds, "no, my boy, in this case we will actually resort to using superior brain power." He points to his noggin'. "Use this thing for something other than a hat rack!" he exclaims. "We shall use the incline plane." Dad runs into the garage and comes back with two 2 x 4's. "Gravity is our friend!" He sets the ends of 2 x 4's on the edge of the roof of the car, in line with the roof rack cross beams, with the length of them sloping down into the pea stone driveway. "Harry (one of his nicknames for me), you stand on those ends of the 2 x 4's so they don't slip out. I'll take the stern and Elna (that's mom), would you take the bow?" Mom is watching this all take shape. She is skeptical, nonetheless, she nods her head.

"I'll help you get it started," adds dad. Clearly hivalry is not dead as he prances around and helps mom get the bow of the boat started off the rack. He then goes around to the stern. "The idea is, we let the 2 x 4's take the weight and let the boat slide down. Got it?" he asks.

We all glance at each other as dad hefts the stern off the rack. First one side of the boat slides onto the 2 x 4's and mom and dad continue guiding it off the car, and then, and then, the weight is too much for mom and her end comes flying at me. This is not good. Two broken ankles are not on my list of things to do today so I jump out of the way. The 2 x 4's slide out and dad loses his end and in a flash the whole thing comes falling down, and mom and dad leap away. CRASH! When the dust clears, the Starcraft sits on the ground, we're all ok, the Peug has a couple new scratches and dad says, "There. Worked like a charm!"

"Guess we have a few bugs to work out of the system," says dad. We get the engine out of the trunk and lug it and the boat into the garage. And there the boat will sit on blocks for the next few weeks until school is out. This is not unlike having a new pair of sneakers. I go out to the garage now and then to check on the boat. I stand there, look at it, study it and dream. If I could put it under my pillow I would.

. . .

Ah, spring turns to summer and there will be freedom. The warden, no, the principal, will release the balls and chains, give us back our personal effects in manila envelopes, there will be no $10 bill, and after the magnesium incident there will, for me, be no bus ticket. But he will unlock the doors and let us out, *free!* We will pour onto the streets. Local upright standing citizen bystanders will watch with horror, the swarm, all with 180 days of pent-up kid behavior as they take over the town. Once home I shed the black and white stripe jump-suit, shed the shoes and don t-shirt and shorts. June, July and August: the three best things about being a ward of the public school system.

The big day comes and we head for the lake. Not surprising, it's an adventure. It's always an adventure, but this time with the boat on top of the mighty Peug, it's all about the humming and whistling and buzzing. A sonic wave precedes us, flocks of birds scatter in terror, mamma bears look up, their faces filled with concern and then quickly herd their roly-poly cubs deep into the woods. Stampedes of zebra and emu... We on the other hand are stuck with it. No matter how fast or slow we go, except stopped, the racket drives us nuts. Despite tropical heat and humidity we eventually close the windows, and the Peug does not have "air." Must not get hot in France. Inside the car it is sweltering, sweat pours from dad and me. He dreams of the cold beers in the cooler in the trunk of the Buick. I dream of the sweating glass pitcher of lime Kool-Aid with the smiley face on it. All to myself. And the shortcut through Chichester with its steep hills and sharp corners coming at us all at once, over and over... the Peug rolls like a Navy destroyer taking huge swells broadside. I wouldn't be surprised if we have the inside wheels in the air a few times.

Summer in all it's splendor is fully upon us and we arrive at Robie's and Mr. Robie is glad to see us. He's all excited and talks up a storm and totters and teeters back and forth at a good clip. The Buick has taken a low-rider attitude under the load and dad and I are right behind in the Peug. It's straining too, stuffed to the gills with junk and with the boat on the roof.

Once checked in, our motley caravan creaks and squeaks to our site and when we get there, it is clear something ghastly has happened. The marsh we used to look out over is gone and in its place is a vast expanse of torn up, black mud with displaced clumps of grass and a roughly established shoreline. North

American Wetlands Conservation Act? What? Oh, that will come along in another twenty years, and because, partly, of disasters like this. Even Tippy is upset looking at it, this used to be his prime hunting ground.

While we're pitching the tent Mr. Robie stops by for a visit. "Eh-ya. 'Decided to make a place fuh th' boats," he says. "Lake's got 'nuff swamp as 'tis. 'Maizin whut you can do with sucha smahl tracktah." He smiles and totters. We agree. It is amazing. But we might use some other words first. Like frightening or devastating.

By evening we have the tent set up, complete with "The Bunkers" sign, cots and sleeping bags are ready, mom has the stove fired up and dad sits in a lawn chair drinking a Carling Black Label, which happens to rhyme nicely with one of his favorite expressions, "Off the table Mabel, the two bucks is for the beer." The boat, despite my bringing up the subject with dad about three (hundred) times, is still on top of the Peug. "First thing tomorrow," he says. "And we will be on the lake." Ah, summer. This is the beginning of another summer.

Barb and Pamp are no longer at Robie's. Pamp has found a new summer job caretaking an estate on Lake Winnipesaukee, just outside of Wolfeboro. So we no longer have the perks available to us when they were here. No more private shower, no more solid roof over our heads on a rainy day, no more smells of chile simmering all afternoon.

The next morning, after breakfast dad makes good on his promise and we start up the Peug and drive onto the new "point" where Mr. Robie has created a "launching ramp." The big hummocks of grass, the cat o' nine tails, all the little ins and outs are gone. The *skrigas* are gone. This is my first experience with the loss of a place. I feel sad.

We bump along, listening to the uneven clods of soil and mud hit the underside of the car, and just hope we don't get stuck. The launching ramp is simply a few loads of sand Mr. Robie has dumped into the water. Seeing how we don't have the boat on a trailer, it's not of particular use to us. Maybe not such a bad thing. It looks like a prime spot to get your car stuck.

Given our experience with dad's brilliant incline plane concept, we decide to skip it in favor of enlisting the help of whoever we can into this operation. You ask one or two guys around here for help and before you know it, eight guys are tripping over one another, all clamoring to get in on the fun. And so, just like that, the boat is off the car and sitting by the water's edge. We thank them for their help, and they loiter, they're just getting warmed up, "Sure we can't help you with the engine?" they ask. But this would be pure chaos, eight guys, bunched up, all trying to install a 6 h.p. outboard on a rowboat, so we politely thank them and say, "we're all set." Some of them actually look put out. Funny watching grown men sulk. In ones and twos they wander away.

Dad and I turn our attention to the engine, hooking it over the stern of the boat and carefully tightening the clamps. We then get the gas tank and hose, the fire extinguisher, life preserver cushions, the oars, and a hank of rope and the anchor. And the squeeze bulb horn. With all this stowed away, we stand back and admire the setup. Dad looks at me and grins. "Well Harry, I 'spose we otta go do us sum boatin," he says. "Dontcha think?" And I'm all for it. "Why dontcha go tell yar motha what we're up to," he adds and I bound back to the tent to tell mom we're going boating. Wow! Boating!

Put my dad at the steering wheel of an airplane and he's a picture of methodical, rational, and precise control of the machine. At the controls of any other mechanized device; electric drill, car, can opener, or boat, his approach is a little less than ideal. Each step of the way is prefaced by the question expressed or implied, "Now what do we do?" So we push the boat into the water, I get in and dad gives it a good final shove and hops in. And now we're drifting toward open water. A man and a boy sitting in a boat... now what do we do? "Let's start the engine," says dad. But wait, we need to hook up the fuel tank. Fuel tank... did we put gas in the fuel tank? Fortunately dad did, which is not to say there will be other times, when it was his job, he didn't. Next and most important: did we put oil in the fuel? Yes, we did.

Dad hooks the fuel line to the tank and squeezes the pressure bulb six times, just like Dana Haggett said to do. Then he goes to the engine and hooks up the other end and gas sprays all over the place. Make note: hook up both ends of fuel line before squeezing pressure bulb six times. With the line secure at both ends, dad then has me squeeze the bulb a few more times. We continue to drift out to sea. Dad looks at the engine, like it's going to say something, but of course it's quiet, exceedingly quiet. "Well, let's see," says dad. He lowers the prop into the water and folds down the tiller. "Set throttle to start. Check," he says. "Pull out choke. Check. Pull starter cord. Check." He looks at me. "Harry, you ready for this?" he asks.

I'm not sure what it is I need to be ready for but say, "Yes."

Dad pulls the starter cord a couple times. The little engine putters but does not start. We drift. Dad looks at the engine. "Let's reduce the choke," he says. "Don't want to get her flooded." He pushes in the choke half way. He gives the starter cord a good healthy yank and the engine roars into life and the prop pops up backwards out of the water. Dad hits the kill button. We are engulfed in a cloud of oily blue smoke and all is again, quiet. I hope no one's watching this. The smoke clears and he looks at me, impishly. "Harry," he says, "a couple things we might want to add to the preflight checklist: make sure engine is in neutral, and see that it's locked into the down position. Got that?"

"Aye-aye, sir," I say, and snap off a crisp salute. So dad fiddles with the controls. We've now drifted out of the cove. We're over the sandbar, the boat pitches in the waves.

"Bettah get this thing stahted," he says. "Harry would ju squeeze that bulb anutha time ah two?" he asks and I do. He pulls the starter cord and the little engine starts. It starts, it runs and dad gives it a moment and pushes in the choke. He throttles it down and snaps it into forward and off we go.

There are moments when a person's map of life changes entirely. Sometimes we don't know it and sometimes we do. And for me, under way in the boat, my map turns all around and I know it. Dad and I are on the water. There is sunlight and open space and the water itself. Our surroundings are dynamic, the possibilities are endless. The boat feels solid and capable, and the little 6 h.p. thrums along. And I know it, the instant dad faces me what he's going to say, and he asks, "Would you like to take the controls?"

"Yes!" I say, jumping up from my seat. Dad slows the engine and puts it in neutral, and we trade seats. The engine idles, putt, putt, ding, ding, ding.

"Before we get going," he says, "there are a few things to remember. One, watch where you're going. Two, if another boat approaches on your starboard, he has right of way. On your port, you have rights. And sailboats, canoes, and rowboats always have the right of way." He studies my face. "As do swimmers. You don't want to run over a swimmer. Do you have that?" he asks.

"Sort of," I say. The right of way thing is a little confusing, but the part about swimmers, I got that. "Dad, how did you know about right of way?"

"Same as with airplanes," he says. "We'll work on it. You'll get it."

I look at the engine, and the controls don't make any sense. Dad sits next to me for a moment and explains what they do and then moves to the middle seat. I snap the engine into forward and give it some gas, a lot of gas actually and the stern of the boat whips to the side and we fly around in a circle. "Harry!" yells dad, "slow'er down!" and I look at the controls. Which is the throttle? This one, and I grab the tiller and give the handle a twist and we go even faster! "Tutha way Harry!" yells dad, and I turn it the other way and thank goodness the boat slows and settles in the water. "That was kinda 'citin," says dad. "Now push tha tillah to tutha side," he adds, and I do and we straighten out. My heart races, and all of a sudden I feel like I need to pee. "Jahzuz Harry we almost lostah," says dad, but he's got a big grin on his face. And I realize a boat is a very lively thing.

It's a little confusing, pushing the tiller to the left to turn to the right. Then another boat pops out from shore and is going really fast, it's towing a skier and is coming from my left. "Who has right of way?" asks dad.

"I don't know!" I yell, anxious about what to do. And like magic the oncoming boat veers to his right and passes by us.

"You do, Harry," says dad, and the people in the speedboat wave and we wave back. O.K., I'm kinda getting this. It seems like a lot of work, a lot to be thinking about. "But don't take it for granted other boaters know the rules or are paying any attention," dad adds. I can see there's big responsibility in

132

being at the helm. "How about we go back and see if your mother and Vic would like to go out?" asks dad.

At speed I turn the boat back toward Robie's in a broad sweeping arc and open up the throttle. We are flying... compared to being out with Harvey. The boat bounces through the waves but feels secure, it's made to do this. Spray leaps up from the bow, it's thrilling. We come back to Robie's cove and I slow down and we putter in. My steering skills are still a little sketchy, we wander way back and forth, but manage to not hit anything or run over swimmers. Beaching the boat, likewise is a little iffy.

I point the boat for shore. "Steady as she goes, Harry," says dad. "Now giver a little gas, that way she'll slide up on shore..." and I give it more than a little, "That's a bit too much!" shouts dad, "Shut her down! Shut her down!" Shore is coming up real quick. "Pull up the motor!" yells dad. "Shut her down!"

And I am totally confused and flustered and I do manage to slow down the throttle, but we have momentum... and WHAM! We hit shore and the bow flies up and onto the grass and the motor is still chugging at it, it's still in gear and I'm struggling to get it pulled up but it's locked down and... I'm about to burst into tears... and I feel a hand on my shoulder and it's dad. "Harry," he says calmly, "let me help you," and I hop out into the water and he fiddles with the engine and gets things all hunky dory. I am shaking with adrenaline. "No harm done Harry, nothing to worry about," he says.

We are walking back to the tent and dad says, "Orville, remember this: any landing you can walk away from is a safe one." Mom and Vic are at the beach. By the time we get over there, I've had a chance to calm down.

Mom looks up from her book. "How'd you do?" she asks.

"Fine," says dad, and I'm relieved to hear him say it. "There's a few things to figure out..."

"It was great!" I interrupt. "Mom, it's so cool being out there. And the boat is fast!" She looks at dad with a slight wave of concern. I catch dad shaking his head and gives me a look that says, "keeping quiet on this would be a good idea."

We have BLT's for lunch. This year we have a toaster Auntie Tora gave us and dad's been put in charge of making toast. In theory, it's a neat little unit; a sheet metal pyramid, the sides are perforated and there's a lip around the bottom. Well, see, you set this over a lit burner on the stove and rest a slice of bread on each side and... you better keep an eye on them. The idea is, and don't we know we all have great ideas, the bread toasts on one side and you flip over the slices and then toast the other side. And well, what you get in actual practice is slightly different than the idea. You get slices of bread burned to a crisp on the bottom edges and not toasted at all on the tops. Some say carbon in your diet is a good thing. I hope they're right. Whenever we have toast by dad, we have carbon.

After lunch we gather our goodies for a swim. Amazing, the pile of junk. Towels, floppy hats, bottles of sunscreen, flippers, masks and snorkels, cold drinks. And the ladder. You'd think we're heading out on a week long expedition. The boat, *my* boat, O.K., our boat, waits, pulled up on shore. We pile our junk into it and naturally, I take the back seat, the seat where the captain of the ship sits. Dad looks at me. "Harry, are you ready to do this?" he asks. Mom and Vic look at me, a bit skeptical.

"Yes," I say. But mom and Vic have already taken their seats mid-ships and dad is left standing on shore. "Harry, would you give us a push in?" I ask my dad. He calls me Harry, I call him Harry, a name we've chosen from a wide inventory we have for one another. I look at him and grin, after all, he's the dad and I'm the kid and so it's his job to do as I say, right? He looks at me as though he knows exactly what I'm thinking and sticks out his tongue.

We all sit there like bumps on a log and look at him. Dad merely shakes his head. He knows resistance is useless so he starts pushing. With all our weight in the boat, which is now firmly planted on the bottom, it doesn't budge. He struggles and strains and grunts, to no avail. "'Guess you'll all have to get out," he says. We all protest like this is the greatest imposition, but get out. Now he pushes the boat out most of the way with ease. We climb back in and take our seats. Mom and Vic shake wet clumps of muck and pebbles out from between their feet and flip-flops. Tippy does the same thing when he gets muddy feet, except he doesn't wear flip-flops. I just hope neither mom or Vic will lick between their toes. That'd be going just too far. Dad gives the boat one great final push and hops into the bow seat. Everyone looks at me. All at once, this is my show and proudest moment, but I also realize I now have to make good on it. I ask dad to give the pressure bulb on the fuel line a few squeezes and he does. I tilt the engine back, lowering the prop into the water and lock it, make sure it's in neutral, pull the choke out half way, set the throttle to start and yank on the starter cord. Once, twice and thrum! The little thing comes to life, and I push in the choke and it stalls. Oh no... but I repeat the process, the motor starts and I leave the choke out for just a moment. There's quite a cloud of smoke around us, I push in the choke and the engine idles nicely. We've drifted out a bit, I put it in gear and we're under way.

I have to stand up to see over the heads of my passengers. Plus this is cool, the captain of the ship, standing up to see and be seen, putting along at a slow speed, safely seeing his craft out of harbor. I negotiate a slightly smoother course out of the cove, avoiding the shallows and weeds. Long tendrils of bright green water grass lean and wave in the subtle current, and there are lily pads with bright yellow blossoms bobbing on the surface. The occasional frog jumps from his lily pad perch, and dragonflies scatter as we pass.

We get out over the sandbar and Vic says, "Let's go around Triggs Island!" Everyone seems amenable with this so I point the boat toward the island and once over deep water, open up the throttle. Everyone will be so impressed with how fast we're going, flying, hopping and skipping over the waves... but... no. I find the limitations of 6 horse power. The little engine revs, the prop churns, but with four people in the boat, we do not fly. Rather, we plow. My visions of zipping around the island, of wind and waves and spray splashing up and giving us a thrill do not materialize. Instead we plod along for an eternity. All of us are, frankly, bored out of our trees and wishing we were having a swim by the time we get half way around the island.

Around Triggs, a number of buoys stick up through the surface, lurching in the waves. They're wooden posts painted white, the tops of some are painted red, others, black, and what they're telling us is where safe passage can be found through these rock infested waters. "North and east on black, south and west on red," yells dad.

But, not knowing which way is north, let alone the other three directions, this is not especially helpful. "Which way is which?" I call.

Mom points to Triggs Landing, on the shore. "That's north," she says. I look at the shore and think about this. I stand up and study the approaching buoys.

"So… stay between the red and black…?" I ask tentatively.

"That's right," says dad. We pass between the buoys and can see big boulders, all brown and green, forgotten ghosts looming under the water, waiting for the hapless direction challenged boater to come along, waiting for a tasty propeller snack. Around the island there are yet more buoys to figure out. It's like a puzzle, and a compass would be handy. This of course means a trip to Winnipesaukee Motor Craft.

After the long and arduous journey, we're hot and bored and happy to get to the sandbar. We find the spot we've been using, shallow enough to jump out of the boat without being over our heads, and with a beautiful clean sandy bottom. I slow the boat and put it into neutral and dad throws the anchor overboard, letting a length of line play out. I shut off the engine, the quiet rings like a bell. We all sit still for a moment, each soaking it in the feelings of the water and space around us. Mom asks me, "Would you like to give the crawl another try?"

I look her in the eye. "No," I say. "I mean, thanks mom, but no." And the slightest flicker of relief crosses her face.

"You sure?" she asks, halfheartedly. She's being a good sport about it, but we both know it's hopeless.

"Yes," I say. "I want to go snorkeling," and before she gets a chance to encourage again, I'm getting my flippers on. Vic and dad have already leaped into the water.

"I'm going to get comfortable and read for a while," says mom. She gathers the life cushions onto the middle seat, tipping one up against the gunnel for under her shoulders.

I dip my mask and snorkel into the water and spit into the mask and swish it around. This helps keep the glass from fogging up. I put it on and get the mouthpiece in between my teeth. And just like the ultimately cool guys who get to do this for a living with Jacques Cousteau, I sit on the gunnel with my back to the water and roll off back first into the waves. The sounds of splashing water and bubbles echo in my ears, I exhale to clear the snorkel and then, except for my breathing and heartbeat it is quiet. Being underwater, in another world, is the coolest.

Sunlight bends through the water and dances on the bottom. Looking up at the underside of the surface, it's a lively mirror. What's above is unknown. I can see the bright yellow anchor rope off in the distance, sloping into space to the anchor, a giant blue mushroom, leaning on its side, digging into the sand. I swim over to it, take a deep breath and haul myself underwater hand over hand along the rope. The anchor's weight holds me under, I hang there as long as my breath allows, then let go and bob to the surface and kaphooey!, blow the water from the snorkel and then fill my lungs with air. It would not be fun to suck in a passerby dragonfly... I circle the boat and study the hull underwater. Where the surface meets it the water curls and ripples in a thousand little darts of light. Rows of rivets line up along the stem and chines and stern. The lower unit of the engine hangs down. I examine the aluminum prop, a spinning wing, such a small thing which does so much work, and the swept back shapes of the casings. I image them in motion, things of wonder streaming through the water, doing what they're made to do.

I pop up for a look around and see dad lolling around with his back to me. Poor unsuspecting soul. Swimming with flippers is like swimming with rockets strapped to your feet. It's time to have some submarine fun. Just under the surface I swim and steadily build speed right for dad. When I can make out the shape of his body underwater I take a deep breath and dive. He is oblivious to my presence. Bearing down on him I bring my arms forward and at the moment of impact I grab both his ankles and hold on. Part of his shout makes it underwater, I grin a devilish grin around my mouthpiece and pull him off his feet. Just as he starts to flail I let go and dart away, swim another twenty feet and burst to the surface, spitting the snorkel out of my mouth and gulping in air and hooting. But there's little time to recuperate. Dad is bearing down on me, but I have the advantage. I think. He's trying to run while I, the slippery seal have only to dive under and let the flippers do the work.

"Harry... I'm gonna get you!" he hollers, wild faced, bearing down on me. In the excitement I fumble with the snorkel, jamming it into my mouth, here he comes his great hulk... and I dive and kick... but feel his iron grip on an ankle. He's got me! He hauls me back with all his strength. I blubber out a faint scream underwater, I struggle, it's no use. He grabs me, all arms and legs going in all directions, picks me up and bodily tosses me into the air. I fly, disoriented, flailing and splash into the water. I pop up and wave my arms around and scream and go back for more. I dive... this game of submarine sea monster is too much fun. The game changes significantly when dad gets his own flippers and mask and snorkel... but the game goes on for years.

And of course, it's also unbearably funny to sneak up on mom, lounging in the boat, reading her book and savoring a rare moment of peace. Quietly, quietly at the boat's freeboard, I slip underwater and let the snorkel fill with water. Then... shhh... aim the snorkel... and kaphooey! Push every available morsel of air out from my lungs with all my might, and a column of cold lake water leaps into the air, arcs gracefully, disperses and comes down on mom's steaming hot sun-tanning body. Splash! Oh the shrieks, oh the commotion!

After pulling this trick a few times, mom let's me know, "It is not funny and you are not to do it again. Is this clear?" she queries.

I look at her and grin and say, "Yes, mom." And she looks at me like, "don't you dare do it again." But we both know it's her job to draw a line... and it's my job to cross it. And so it should come as no surprise to her the next time I do it, but it did and there are the shrieks and commotions. And mom looks at me, wildness in her eyes, shakes her finger and let's me know what's what in no uncertain terms... and I look at her and grin, and she stops and looks at me and a little smile creeps across her face and I know I've got her. Exasperated, she looks at me and hisses, "Oh! You! You little bastard!" And we laugh and hoot and I wonder if she realizes what she's implying by calling me a bastard.

.   .   .

Bruce Walker is Mr. Robie's stepson, and he and his family have a big trailer permanently set up at the campground. The slinky race boat Bruce has was a gift from Mr. Robie. It's a 3-Star Pigeon Race Boat, it's the jazziest boat on the lake, and Bruce keeps it in beautiful condition. I regard the Pigeon Boat with equal parts awe and fear. It is an unusual design, like a very narrow and low wedge of cheese with a sharply pointed bow. It is double lapstrake planked, and around the transom the planking comes up from the bottom in graceful curves, wraps around the soft chines, and forms something of a deck along the sides of the cockpit. Or to put it more succinctly, I'll throw in one more boat term, and one of my favorites: her transom has extreme tumblehome.

Bruce has it equipped with a 25 horsepower Johnson outboard engine. This engine is a raw, clattering, high performance machine, the epitome of horsepower to weight for its day, with a blade bronze prop with three special tulip shaped blades. Hot stuff.

As a young man, Mr. Robie raced the Pigeon on Lake Winnipesaukee. At the time he had a 60 horsepower engine on it, and in this trim, he won the 1928 Lake Winnipesaukee Outboard Marathon. There's a historic photo of him driving the boat at speed - it's barely touching the water and is putting up no wake. Wildness!

Bruce with his family aboard, leave the cove in the Pigeon, the boat sits low in the water, slithering along, the engine makes quite the mechanical din. The bow pennant with a picture of a tipping martini glass on it waves languidly in the breeze. This is the calm before the storm. They make their way over the sandbar and Bruce opens her up, the clatter turns to a roar and like a shot, the boat leaps forward. Seeing the Pigeon at speed on open water, it's not unlike a bullet. It is a bullet. A streak of white and blue with a small trail of spray behind it, and then it's gonesville.

And Bruce, responsible family man that he is, is not above a few antics. Every once in a while, when he's been out by himself, he will come flying into Wiley Brook at full throttle, the engine shrieking! At the very last possible moment, in the little bit of a cove where Mr. Robie has the barge and swimming beach set up, Bruce quickly turns the boat, as hard over as she'll go, the bow digs into the water and flips the stern up and around and in no space or time at all it turns 180 degrees. And so without skipping a beat, he has turned around and is flying out of the brook... still under full power, and he is gone. Headway speed in the channel? What? I can't hear you!

Bruce also starts water skiers from the barge. Holding the tow rope, his wife Diane, bravely steps into a single ski and waits. Bruce, with an observer in the Pigeon, draws the slack out of the rope and when the tension is just right, Diane yells, "hit it!" And Bruce gives the Johnson full throttle, the stern of the Pigeon digs in and Diane hops off the barge. The boat pulls wildly, Diane sinks in a bit, the tip of her ski is up, plowing water. But the boat is so powerful, this all happens in a second and Rhrrawr! The Pigeon gains speed and is flying toward the lake, Bruce steers the boat through the channel and around the weeds, they are having the times of their lives, Diane slaloms behind the boat, they fly over the sandbar and onto open water, quickly receding into little specks, and disappear.

Eventually my sense of awe for the Pigeon overcomes my fear. I become curious, and the day will come I ride in it. The day will also come I take it out on my own.

My pal and partner in mischief, Dicky, is visiting and one day we decide the little Evinrude isn't running quite as well as it should and endeavor to fix it. We know what we're up to will be frowned upon by the grown-ups so we sneak the boat to the relatively hidden dock up the brook, also by some coincidence the very same dock Bruce ties the Pigeon. The Walkers aren't around so the Pigeon rests under its snug canvas cover.

We have our collection of tools: a well rusted adjustable wrench, a couple of screwdrivers in similarly poor condition, some pliers, maybe a three pound hammer and cold chisel. In short, the tools we have are not well suited to working on an outboard engine, or much of anything except perhaps crushing

142

gravel for highway projects. But fools rush in where angels dare not tread and we pop the cover off the patient and get to work. Pointing at one of the many widgets, Dicky says, "There's the fuel pump. I think that's the problem." He grabs the pliers and yanks off the black rubber hoses connected to it. Gasoline sprays all over the place, a slick rainbow spreads over the surface of the water. I want to get in on the action and grab the adjustable wrench. "Yeah, undo those four bolts," says Dicky. So I squeeze in and turn the bolts. More gas dribbles out of the widget and we're engulfed in a cloud of fumes. Man, I hope no one comes along smoking a cigarette. Huh, I have all the bolts out, but the cover is stuck. Dicky hands me the hammer. Important note: People who call themselves mechanics and know what they're doing almost never use a hammer. Hammer use = brute force. If you have someone working on your engine and you see them pick up a hammer, nine out of ten, get that person away from said engine as quickly as possible. I give the cover a good whack and it falls off, deep into the bowels of the lower housing. And all manner of little springs and steel balls and O-rings and other unnamable thingies go flying in all directions, quite a few of them in the direction of the water and in they go plop, plop, plop, never to be seen again. Dicky and I give each other furtive glances. We know this is trouble, and by extension, we are *in* trouble. Dicky shrugs his shoulders as if to say, 'it's your boat, not mine... not my problem.'

We start with an engine that, O.K., I'll admit it, runs perfectly and we end up with an engine that doesn't run. At all. And we have no hope of putting it back in running order without involving grown-ups. And on top of it all, it's a beautiful summer day. The kind of day a kid would rather be out on the water in his boat, rather than bearing bad news to a grown-up. I hate it when this happens. We leave the mess as is, where is, and reeking of gasoline walk back to the tent. We stay away from people smoking cigarettes. Mom takes one look at us and knows something's up. She puts her hands on her hips.

"Mom," I say, "the boat wasn't running very well so we took it apart."

"You took it apart." she says, alarmed. "All of it?"

"No, just the engine," I say. Dicky is standing off to the side, keeping out of it. "Actually, just the fuel pump. I think. Well, first we turned the knob on the front, but that made it worse."

Mom draws Dicky into the equation with her eyes, and her look is not happy. Rather, her look is she's about to blow a fuse. "And does it run better now?" she asks.

"No," I say.

"Does it run *at all?*" she asks. There's a distinct and troubling edge in the way she asks the question.

"No," I say.

Mom doesn't say anything for a moment, which feels like a year and then says, "Let's have a look at the boat together, shall we?"

This is torture. "O.K." I say. Leaving the tent, she heads in the direction of where we usually keep the boat. "No mom, it's back here," I say and gesture toward the brook. And now I know we're in big trouble because she knows I know we snuck off with it, which means we knew we were not doing the right thing but we did it anyway. I get that shaky feeling in my legs, and a tight feeling in my throat. We walk, no, march to the dock, we march past the swim area where everyone else is having fun. And there's the scene of the crime, the boat, with the cover off the engine, and tools scattered all over the place. Wild hues of purple and green coat the water as gasoline continues to drip from the engine.

"Some parts fell in the water," I squeak. We three stand on the dock.

"So there's no way to put it back together?" asks mom.

"No. I mean yes," I say.

"Well, which is it?" asks mom.

"There's no way," I say. And with this, mom's fuse does in fact blow.

"We start with a perfectly fine running little boat. This, Gordon, is not *your* boat. It is *OUR* boat. And now it does not run. Now none of us can go out on the lake in the boat. And Dicky, you're in trouble too, do you understand?" Dicky obediently nods his head. "Gordon, I want you to pick up this mess and row the boat around to where we keep it. And you two are grounded for the rest of today. I think we'll go grocery shopping." With this she turns and starts to march in the direction of the tent. "Dicky, you come with me." The two of them goose step back to the tent. I can tell mom's giving him an earful. I row the boat with the dead little engine past all the happy swimmers to where we keep it and pull it up on shore.

And now we have to go grocery shopping, undoubtedly with no side trip to Bailey's for an ice cream. I won't even mention this might be a good idea. We have to spend the afternoon in hot stinky town. Yuk! We have to put on shoes! And walk around Hunter's and listen to mom sputter about the prices.

When dad shows up from work he looks hot and sweaty and tired. If ever a man has 'let's take the boat to the sandbar and go for a swim,' written all over him, it would be my dad and it would be right now. He reaches in the cooler and pulls out a cold one. Pffit! He opens it and takes a sip. Mom announces, "*Your* son has something to tell you." Dad looks at me, looks through me. I feel like I need to go to the men's room, instead, I freeze.

"Yes?" asks dad. And he sits himself in a lawn chair.

I tell dad what happened in the most reasonable man to man way I can think of. He doesn't say anything. I stand there. I squirm. But dad's a guy and he understands being curious about machinery and being itchy and wanting to explore. "We'll have to get it fixed, and the cost will come out of your allowance," he says. I droop. This could amount to indentured servitude for the next three years, my legs go weak, and he adds, "After we get it fixed, you will use it only with your mother or me. Until further notice." Oh! He does know how to strike a blow. To the gut. I look at him, like this is in direct violation of the Geneva Conventions but he sits there and takes another sip of his beer and doesn't budge. "I would like to go to the sandbar for a swim," he says, finally. "And I think you two monkeys," he looks at Dicky and me, "can do the rowing." My dad knew how to make it smart and make it stick, and at the same time he knew how to be a good guy. Bless his heart.

"Let's go get the engine off the boat," he says. Dicky gets up. Dad puts his hand on Dicky's head. "Thanks, no, just Harry and me." We walk over to the boat, we don't say anything. Dad let's me help with undoing the clamps that hold the engine onto the transom. He catches my eye and holds it. "You've learned a lesson?" he asks. This is man to man.

"Yes, sir," I say. We continue for a moment in quiet. I coil the fuel line on top of the tank.

"Good," he says. He nods and rests his hand on my head. "That's good. Now let's go for a swim."

It is widely known around the campground that Bruce is the Doctor of Motors. When he and his family show up the next weekend, dad has a chat with Bruce about the Evinrude, and Bruce agrees to have a look at it. I think there is offer of payment, which he undoubtedly refuses. In the end, a six-pack or two of Genesee Cream Ale probably find their way into his refrigerator. Beer is a great form of currency among men.

Standing under the pines near our campsite, dad, Bruce and I have a look at the engine. "Indeed, it is the fuel pump," says Bruce. "Did you try to start it after you took it apart?" he asks.

"No, sir," I say. Bruce is a big barrel of a guy with a lot of hair on his back. He has a kind way about him and is quick to share his wide, easy smile. I can tell as he looks at the engine, he's in his element. A breeze off the lake blows his hair in his face and he pushes it aside. "You'll need a..." and he rattles off a list of parts. "I'm going over to Winnipesaukee Motor Craft anyway," he says and he turns to me. "Want to come along?"

Just because he knows at first sight exactly what to do about the engine, and the way he says the name of the marina, quick and precise, I know I want to go. I look at dad. "That'd be fine," he says.

A little later, Bruce comes by in his Buick Estate Wagon. This car is so big, from stem to stern it stretches into the neighboring county. With his two older sons Matt and Paul, who are about my age, I hop in and off we go. Matt and Paul and I have palled around some, but this is a field trip. We immediately start goofing around and in no time Paul has everyone screaming with laughter. All about goofy little stuff, but nonetheless a riot when Paul puts his crazy spin on it. The big Ocean Liner Buick floats over the roads. All of us are in hysterics.

Lake Winnipesaukee is a very different scene from Lake Wentworth. It's some 14 times the size, a number of towns dot its shores and most of the summer places on it are big and high dollar. So it follows, the boats on the lake are in the same class; big and fancy, high dollar and usually, fast.

Pulling into the marina, my eyes go wild. Boats are lined up in the yard, some on cradles, others on trailers and then there are sheds filled with boats, their bows peek out from the cool shade. The place is a beehive of activity, men are operating trucks and fork lifts and an overhead crane moving boats in and out of the water. This is the big time, and even though we are small potatoes, Bruce walks into the store with a sense of ease, and I do my best to emulate this. We are boat guys. The displays of boating gear in the store rival the penny candy counter at The Old Country Store. That's saying something, or maybe I'm growing up. Every kind of rope you can think of, beautiful marine hardware, compasses, instruments of all description, lighting, bright and shiny engines, the outboards in their slick housings, the inboards you can see the whole thing, the engine itself with various tubings and wires and linkages all painted and beautiful. All those many mechanical parts, all brand new and ready to go, lie within. Ready to turn the alchemy of internal combustion into a thrilling ride, flying with ease across the lake. All those components and technologies, miracles of accumulated experience, design and good intention. All of it, just for the fun of it. Amazing.

We head over to the parts counter and Bruce guides me through purchasing the small handful of thingies we need to put the little Evinrude back into running order. I pull out my bucking bronco wallet and pay. It feels good to be doing this, the act of taking responsibility and putting things right. The parts guy hands me my change and a half dozen little craft paper envelopes with numbers written on them, and he hands me a detailed receipt, a sheet of yellow paper with blue carbon writing on it. Bruce buys the parts he needs for his projects and we're on our way.

But not so fast. Now it's time we wander around the yard. This is the first of many such occasions with Bruce. He discounts the fiberglass boats as "plastic pigs," and the aluminum as "beer cans." I wonder why he has been tolerant of having anything to do with our aluminum boat, perhaps he's being polite, or maybe he sees potential in me that I might have a real boat some day. We breeze past the plastic pigs and beer cans and head for the sheds, where the wooden boats reside. And we step into another world, a world of elegant design and craftsmanship.

The boats loom in the cool shade, the metal sheds tick in the sun's heat, and rumble in the breeze. Smells of pungent motor and gear oil, spicy mahogany and varnish and fumy gasoline fill the air. Shafts of sunlight pour through minute holes and seams in the metal siding, beams glow in the dust we stir up. Bruce starts pointing out details. The difference between a hard chine and a soft one, a planning hull and a displacement hull, carvel and lapstrake planking, skegs, rudders, props. Tumblehome. A plumb stem as opposed to a cutter. It is fascinating, and I am a sponge. We look at the lines, the complex sweeping curves. And the names: Chris Craft, Gar Wood, Hacker, Century, Thompson, Lyman, Penn Yan, Goodhue Hawkins. They reflect the names of the people who first envisioned them, they reflect another time. I learn to use my eyes, I learn about discernment, what fineness is. And I fall in love with the old wooden boats.

Driving back to Robies, I start on a list of about a thousand questions, and Bruce is happy to answer them. "Wood is a living organism," he says. "It's naturally buoyant and it has give. You ride in a wooden boat, then a plastic pig. You'll feel the difference."

We manage the summertime Saturday snarl called Wolfeboro and stop at Pop's Donuts. Sugar coated crullers, let's hear it for saturated fat! The glazed chocolate crullers... just the right amount of crispiness on the outside and the rest melts in your mouth. Jelly donuts... pots of coffee. The store is a small space Pop carved out of his barn, with a modest glass front display case. Simple and good. And down the line, Pop would add fudge to his offerings and for some reason, Paul is gonzo for it. Well-sugared and caffeinated we hit the road. It's getting hot, and we want to get back to the lake.

Bruce has a plan for fixing the Evinrude. We put the engine back on the Starcraft, row it to the scene of the crime and there we take the whole rig out of the water on his trailer and tow it to his campsite. This is where Bruce has his tools, not to mention he's hesitant to work on a boat when it's in the water. It's a good way to lose tools - and parts as I learned - overboard. We jump through these hoops and we've got the boat at his site.

The Doctor of Motors follows a particular protocol for best results. Back the patient up to the end of the picnic table. Get the Kennedy tool box, hoist it on top of the table and open it up. Neat rows of sockets and wrenches live in there as do a selection of screwdrivers and pliers and other interesting things. Bruce is a guy who will take a brand new screwdriver and give the tip his own special grind. It's a hollow grind so it is just the very edge of the tip which grips in the screw head. Bruce spreads out clean cotton tea towels to set tools and things on as he works. He then goes inside the trailer to change into the proper attire and get a cold Genesee Cream Ale.

When he emerges from the trailer he is wearing flip-flops, plaid bathing trunks and a sunflower yellow double breasted chef's jacket with matching toque. Remember, Bruce is a big round guy. He cut's quite a profile, and his manner is fitting as a *Chef de cuisine*, or *motors* as the case may be. He is well practiced, methodical and nothing rattles him. Nothing that is, unless he opens the toolbox and finds things have wandered away and not been put back. By, could it be… where did Matt and Paul go, anyway? This makes him crazy. But if all is well in the tool box, he opens the cream ale, *Pfitt!* and takes a good mouthful from it. "Ahhh…!" he exclaims. "And what do we have here?" He pops the cover off the engine, looks and pokes at things and goes to work. The little envelopes of parts are lined up on one of the tea towels. Bruce does a little of this and a little of that, he wrenches, scrapes, puts on a bit of the proper sealant and reassembles. He talks about the relative merits of motor oils, Permatex Form-a-Gasket and Never Seize. He's an enthusiast and an optimist, and there are many things mechanical in the world which simply amaze him. While he works he explains things, we talk, ponder and debate, and in no time, the fuel pump is back together. Bruce takes the opportunity to fiddle with a few other things he feels require his attention. Grease the throttle and gear shift mechanisms, inspect and clean the spark plugs, expound on the effects of air to fuel ratio and different heat range spark plugs on the properties of combustion… and with Kool-Aid in hand, I am soaking it up.

When he's finished he starts the engine. Outboard motors don't exactly have mufflers. They simply vent the exhaust under water and this deadens the sound. Out of water it's, BRAAAP!, POP, POP! RHARRR! It's deafening but we grin listening to it. These engines also pick up their cooling water from the lake, so we shut it down in less than a minute. I am pleased and relieved it's running again.

Satisfied with his work, Bruce says, "Let's put this little vixen in the water and take it for a spin. We might want to adjust the mixture under load..." So we toss the Starcraft back in the water and go out to zoom around the sandbar, zoom being a relative term. Bruce fiddles with a few things and the engine runs better than it ever has. We put back into the cove, both of us happy and Bruce examines the way the boat's put together. He says, "For a beer can, it's nicely done."

The weather has turned particularly hot and humid. "Hotnuf t' breed minks," says Mr. Robie. I've spent a lifetime wondering if minks require high ambient temperatures to do the deed. Some day I'll look into it. Whether minks are feeling particularly amorous on this day is unknown, but it is hot. Sweltering. Dad's left for work and we've had breakfast and we look at one another. No air is moving and the sun is coming around on the tent. We're all sweaty and limp.

"Let's get out on the lake," says mom. "It has to be cooler out there, and if it's not, we'll just jump in." This sounds like a good idea. Vic looks up from her copy of *Seventeen* and nods her head. Tippy is spread out on the floor of the tent which always stays cool, and for the moment he's found the shadiest corner. He doesn't say anything but just lays there and pants. Must be tough having a perma-press fur coat on days like this. We're already in our suits, so we gather up our stuff and head for the boat. The bare metal gunnels are already too hot to touch, as are the seats, but we have the life cushions to sit on. We're arranging our junk and mom says, "Today, *I'd* like to drive the boat." I giver her a look, like, what?, and see the fire in her expression. She's already got her teeth on the bit, and that she's going to successfully drive the boat is a foregone conclusion. She smirks at me. So there. "Will you show me how to start the engine?" she asks.

I'm about to ask, 'are you sure?' but remember when dad was painting the house last fall and the ladder wasn't quite tall enough for him to reach the very top within his comfort zone. Funny, for a guy who spent so much of his life above 30,000 feet, he was scared of heights. Mom looked at him, exasperated and said, "I'll do it." I was shocked and was about to say something smart when dad looked at me, shook his head and said, "Boy, *never* underestimate the powers of a woman." This was the best piece of advice he ever gave me. Mom grabbed the bucket of paint and the brush from dad, climbed up the ladder to the very tippy-top and clung there like a spider, and painted right up to the peak. She then sprinted down the ladder and with great satisfaction, handed dad the bucket and brush and said, "There."

So I say, "Yes." We're milling around, all about to melt. "Let's push the boat out a bit and you and Vic get in. I'll hold it while you're starting the engine." So we push it out and the two of them get in. I wade out to be by mom to show her what to do. I have her lower the prop into the water and have Vic squeeze the fuel bulb a few times. Then I give mom instructions, step by step and she follows them to a T. Now it's the moment of truth. She yanks on the starter cord. As her clenched hand comes back, she almost clouts me in the jaw. The engine putters but doesn't start. I take a step back. Again with all her strength she pulls on the starter cord. Her boobs threaten to fly out of her bathing suit.

You might be wondering if I have a fixation on my mother's boobs. As a boy who is taking notice of girls, I have a general interest in boobs and that interest is growing. However, I do not have a fixation on my mother's boobs. There are two things to keep in mind. One, with my mom, they are a... um... prominent feature. And two, she does sport a preference for low cut bathing suits. So there is a real possibility in some rare instances her boobs may in fact come flying out. A few of us might find this funny and worthy of mention; a few of us might not. But I digress.

Again the engine sputters but not quite enough. Mom looks at me. Beads of sweat run down her forehead. All of a sudden I'm glad she's the one, in this heat, doing the work. I'm tempted to point this out but say, "Try pushing in the choke. It's so hot, it may not need it." She does and she pulls the cord one more time and the little engine fires and pops and dings and makes a big blue cloud of smoke and mom turns to me, smiling. Pleased as punch she says, "You have no idea what I'm capable of." This, I will find through a lifetime of surprises to be the truth. I push us out, hop in and sit in the bow. This little excursion might turn out to be some fun, after all.

Mom guides the boat through the weeds and onto the lake. She opens the throttle, but with the three of us aboard, it doesn't make a whole lot of difference. Just more noise. Nonetheless, the brim of her big floppy hat flaps back in the breeze. At the helm she is full of adventure, on these high seas she exudes alpha feminism. My mother, given a different set of life circumstances, could easily have become a pirate.

. . .

After an eternity, the "further notice" arrives and I am again allowed to use the boat on my own.

Depending on the time and the day, the lake can take on vastly different character, from glass to breaking waves and everything in between. Out on the water at dawn, the air is cool, the sky grey, and typically the surface is glass. Amazing, when such a large and fluid thing can be perfectly still. Loons will be out at this time of day, singing their haunting songs, or paddling along quietly. Without warning they may dive and swim for great distances underwater, to pop up way off in some direction. Fun to watch them and wonder where in the morning calmness they'll come up. Alone in the boat, going along at full clip, momentarily I close my eyes and lose all sense of motion. It could be I am sitting still with the world moving beneath me.

With the sun up and the atmosphere heating, so comes the wind. It may stir up a light chop, but the stronger it blows the larger the waves, and when blowing hard from the west, down the entire length of the lake, by the time the waves get to the east end they're big rollers moving fast, with breaking whitecaps of foam. When the water is this stirred up, I purposely go east to play in those waves. Traveling with them, I throttle the engine back to climb the windward side, and teetering on the crest open the throttle, plunging the bow into the next. Big sheets of water spray up as the bow buries under power. The deeper you plunge a boat into the water, the more water it displaces and so it becomes more buoyant... and up it pops like a cork. To a point. The trick is to bury the bow but not so deep as to take on water. That'd be bad.

Traveling against the waves is altogether different. Under full power the boat leaps off the crest of a wave and the wind catches underneath it, lifting it higher. Boats have been known to flip over backwards this way, but the little Starcraft falls back crashing into the next advancing wave. Spray ejects from the sides of the hull and gets whipped back, and then up again and down. Bang! The faster I go the wilder it becomes, the boat and pilot frankly, take a beating. It's great and compelling adventure to get a boat high into the air. Waay up.

Weather can be sunny and benign and on the water everything is jolly, or unpredictable and severe. Thunderstorms can come up fast.

I'm on the far side of the lake, all's right with the world but then hear a faint first rumble of thunder. To the northeast, over the Ossipee Range, giant cumulus clouds are building. Glancing at them, faint flickers of lightning appear and a moment later the rumble, but this time it's louder, more distinct. And in a few moments, everything is happening faster, the wind picks up and the air chills.

With the storm approaching, I am forced to make a choice. Stay put? Make a run for home? Make a run for the closest shore? Considering the wind and where the storm is located, I make a run for the nearest shore. Each storm is different, and after dealing with a few of them, I get the hang of it. As an adult, how to read my surroundings is a skill I use all the time, whether I'm out in nature or at a cocktail party.

Putting in on unfamiliar shore is always an adventure, to find a spot far enough from people's camps and land the boat sometimes among rocks, then haul the boat up and out of the water. Then simply sit in the woods with the storm approaching, watching it come across the water, the wind picks up, thunder and lightning crash around, sometimes striking too close for comfort, to sit through it all, to watch it unfold, the turmoil on the water, all the while exposed to the cold and wind is humbling. And then it passes, it becomes calm, how wet and fresh everything is. Droplets of water hang on leaves, a puff of air is all that's needed to break them free. They hit the ground. Birds come out from cover and start chirping, singing. And when all is clear, I slip the boat back into its element and am on my way.

The first time or two I get back from staying out through a storm, mom expresses her concern. But after this, she was confident I know what I'm doing. It probably pleases her, probably reminds her of her own childhood, growing up on Cotton Mountain, being out in nature. Even as a kid mom hunted to put food on the table and always came home with game. In all those experiences she learned the ways of her surroundings.

These days in conversations with various folks, from time to time I'm hearing the term, "helicopter parents," and immediately know what is meant. I've seen a few of them in action, constantly hovering over their kids. How children learn to do *anything* for themselves, let alone how to take care of life's less than rosy moments I don't know.

.   .   .

It's cause for great excitement when the Texas Contingent shows up for a visit. This would be mom's sister Ann, her husband Mike and their three kids, Paula, Miles and Jason. Given we find people from Vermont exotic, these folks are off the chart. They talk funny, and coming from a place where it's summer and they can be outdoors year-round, they are more tan than any of us could ever hope to be. And they are from Corpus Christi, on the *Gulf of Mexico*. They go to Padre Island where there are jellyfish and Portuguese man of wars... Uncle Mike hunts wild pigs called javelinas and has close encounters with rattlesnakes. We are talking The Wild West! He tells stories of encounters out in the brush with illegal immigrants from Mexico, these people have nothing, they wander out of the desert in the middle of the night and Uncle Mike let's them sit around his fire and he feeds them pinto beans, and they are grateful. Uncle Mike smokes cigars and the end of one of his thumbs is missing. He jokes a rattlesnake bit it off and my eyes go wide and then he fesses up and says he lost it in an accident at work... which is fixing helicopters for the Navy.

Aunt Ann is tall and blonde and beautiful, and is full of fun zany ideas. She's high energy and up for anything. It's as though we have visitors from another country, they are that different. Or from another planet.

They show up in their spotless blue Chevy Impala. How they can drive cross country and not get even one bug splattered on the car is a mystery. And not for lack of air conditioning with the windows open. It's mid-summer, and pushing ninety degrees and ninety percent humidity and we're all limp and melting, but to them this is a walk in the park. When they left Corpus it was more like a hundred and five and 99 percent humidity. Uncle Mike is one of the few grownups I know who mostly goes barefoot, and this of course makes him even cooler.

"Ha-ell," says Uncle Mike. He pulls the well chewed stump of a cigar from his mouth and beams. "This all's a coool spring day!" He's not even sweating. "Yawl don't know what *hot* is. I wish I had me a sweater to put on so I don't tayk a cheel."

Uncle Mike pulls two big cans of jalapeño peppers from the trunk of the car. They're from Mexico, the labels are bright yellow and red with all the words are in Spanish. They're a gift mostly for mom, she's the only one of us who'll eat them, and she's all excited. Mom hands Mike our dinky little can opener and he stands at the picnic table and slowly works his way around the can. Mom stands at his side, drooling with anticipation. Fumes waft up from the can and are enough to get Mike to break a sweat, literally. Beads of sweat trickle down his face. With the cover off, he and mom each pluck out one of the dull green peppers and eat them like chunks of cucumber. They munch them down, and hoot and gasp and wheeze. Their faces turn red and they sweat and laugh and remark how good these things are and let's have another one! The rest of us watch this display of masochism and give each other worried looks, and hope they don't spontaneously burst into flames, which seems like a real possibility.

In one fell swoop our merry band grows from four to nine, and Ann and mom manage to keep us all fed. "We're cookin' big, honey!" they cackle to one another, sisters in their element with a common cause: feed the madding, ravenous hordes. That they accomplish this with no real kitchen and no real refrigeration is remarkable. Scrambled eggs, bacon, potatoes, tortillas with melted cheese, coffee, milk, OJ, for nine from a couple of coolers and a two burner camp stove, no problem. The two of them set to it, there's all manner of clattering, eggs go one way, egg shells the other, and bingo, bango bongo, there it is. Come and get it! We swoop in and in a matter of minutes, there's only crumbs left. All is quiet as we stuff our hungry faces. For us kids, right after finishing a meal we jump up and are off for the next adventure. Uncle Mike observes a pattern: eat giant quantities of food, then run around like wild animals. Repeat. After breakfast one morning, we are about to take off. He sits there picking his teeth with the point of his pocket knife, and smiles and shakes his head. He looks at us with eyes twinkling, and says, "Gol dang, nex time after a feed we gonna chain yawl to a tree!" I look at him, wondering if we've done something wrong and he adds, "That way yawl wont eat us outta house and home!" And he laughs and we take off.

One morning, it's coming up on lunch time, or maybe I'm just hankering for a snack, I hover around the campsite. It must be hunger, there isn't any other real reason to hang around. Uncle Mike, being a Texan and knowing how to survive hellaciously hot weather moves slow. He has an easy-going, we're never in a rush way about him. This is completely opposite of how we New Englanders behave. A critical method for surviving winter is to keep moving, and apparently we don't know enough to slow down when the weather turns hot. So I descend on the campsite wondering if it's lunchtime yet, and find out it's not. But if I can wait, lunch will be happening in about a half hour. So, I do my best to sit still. Dad and Uncle Mike are hanging out talking about grown-up stuff. Uncle Mike is sitting in a shady place on one side of the picnic table and he has his pocket knife out. He's digging the crud from underneath his toenails with it. There's nothing out of the ordinary or repulsive about this. Camping is if anything, casual. When he finishes, he folds the knife and puts it in his pocket.

Time passes at a snail's pace and eventually mom and Aunt Ann begin assembling lunch. Not unlike hyenas, the rest of the tribe starts showing up on the scene, we've got the scent, we circle, we salivate, we bare our canines at one another. The tension builds for the kill. And mom and Aunt Ann get the hint and shortly all the fixings for sandwiches are laid out, along with a giant bowl of macaroni salad. We dive in. Moving around the table, putting my Dagwood together, I growl at cousin Miles, letting him know he better not touch that slice of ham. Uncle Mike is across the table perusing the condiment section. There's mayo and mustard and relish and a jar of mom's homemade bread and butter pickles. There's also a dish of sliced jalapeño peppers, which the sane of us stay clear away from. Uncle Mike is looking this way and that for something. It turns out he's looking for a knife with which to apply mustard to his sandwich. Not finding one, he reaches into his pocket, pulls out his pocket knife, opens it, dips the blade into the mustard, puts mustard on his sandwich and goes back for some more. Satisfied, he licks the blade clean, folds the knife and puts it in his pocket. He moves on to the jalapeños.

I stand there, transfixed by what I've seen. Just moments ago, yes, he used the very same blade for removing his toe-jam. I don't know what to say or do, and from experience have found when this is true it's best to say and do nothing. Except in this case, avoid the mustard.

When the Texas Contingent is visiting, picking blueberries on Cotton Mountain is one of the family's favorite activities. That is, all of the family except me. There are places on Cotton Mountain which burned long long ago, and with the soil being so thin, trees are slow to come back. They're still pretty much clearings, but this it turns out is prime blueberry habitat. We head up a narrow dirt road with old stone walls on both sides to one of our favorite spots. Trees tower over us, the canopy forms a tunnel we drive through. The clearing is near an old farm, the house is well kept, it's a simple place, clapboarded sides painted white with green trim, and a porch along the front. It's always so quiet here it's hard to tell if it's occupied. We park the car and get out. We notice there's an old man lying on a day bed on the porch. A very old man, pale and gaunt. He's lying very still, his mouth is open. He lies there so still, we have to wonder is he taking a nap, or is he dead? There's a genuine possibility he's the latter. We decide if he is dead, there's not a lot we can do for him, and if he's asleep we don't want to disturb the old guy, so we sneak by without making a sound. I've always wondered about that old man. It would be pretty creepy if he... it... was... a corpse.

Picking blueberries is so boring, I get down on my hands and knees and pick a berry and put it in my bucket. I look in the bucket. One lonely berry, rolling around making a hollow blueberry in plastic bucket sound. I pick one more berry. After an hour of this I might have thirty berries. Woo-hoo! Enough for a mouthful! Because the process is so slow and frustrating I forget the bucket and resort to picking and eating. I admit, I'm into immediate gratification. When everyone else has had enough of this tedium, which takes an eternity, we gather up back at the car. Mom and Aunt Ann tie for the most berries in their buckets and I win the booby-prize for the least. The old guy on the day bed hasn't moved a muscle.

"Why so few berries?" asks mom. In one of the very rare instances when I'm not trying to be a brat, I stick out my tongue. "So it seems you've already eaten your share... no blueberry pancakes for you, then?" She looks at me and smiles, like this is the most reasonable thing in the world.

"I guess not," I say.

On the way back to Robie's we stop at Auntie's. When the Texans visit, they stay at her house. She is a brave woman who loves her family. This morning she looks a little frazzled and the house is, well... It's a small place, and accommodating five guests, three of whom are rambunctious kids, suffice it to say, the house looks like a tornado went through it. But Auntie is glad to have the berries we give her. She's going to make a cobbler with them which she'll bring when she comes to Robie's this evening for a cookout. Barb and Pamp will be coming and Aunt Connie and her son Whitney too.

Family cookouts are complete madness. The largely unchecked consumption of alcohol has something to do with this. The crowd has now swelled to fourteen and by five o'clock cars encircle our campsite like Conestoga wagons pulled off for the night along The Old Santa Fe Trail. Let's not forget, this is America. There's three big hunks of American Iron, including Whitney's snarling bright red hotrod all jacked up on big tires. Thank goodness for the small sanities from Europe, with representatives from Sweden, Germany and France. *Vive la France!*

We grab a second picnic table from an unoccupied site, great quantities of food appear like magic. Auntie brings the blueberry cobbler, Barb brings a big cauldron of her chili (no aspic salad, thank God), and homemade strawberry shortcakes, and mom and Aunt Ann have already been "cookin' big, honey!" The picnic tables strain under their loads. Dad has a campfire started for roasting corn and potatoes and now throws a match at the starter fluid saturated hibachi... it ignites with a poof! and a tower of flames jumps into the air. He's in charge of incinerating hamburgers and hotdogs. And there's tossed salad, macaroni salad and potato chips and a thousand other good things.

And the booze. Growing up around a bunch of alcoholics, or people who drink too much or whatever they are - I gave up a long time ago trying to figure it out - could be not so great. All fine people and remarkably functional, but nonetheless lessened by being drunk so much of the time. It was a loss. There are times however, when the grown-ups get a little crazy it can be very funny. Embarrassing stories get told, and little comments with stingers on them fly about. Some get ignored, some responded to in turn. Occasionally someone will get thrown in the lake, and card games played late into the night get loud and rowdy.

Just before dinner Aunt Ann gets going about Whitney's car, it is just too red with too much chrome and way too loud. Somehow she gets ahold of the keys and starts it up. She hoots and hollers and revs the engine, and the exhaust is extremely loud. Good thing she didn't actually go tearing around in it. We stand there, watching the spectacle and egg her on. Finally she shuts it off, gets out of the car and hollers some more. Everywhere else in the campground you can hear a pin drop. Terrorized campers peer out from behind pine trees. No one knows what to do or what to expect next. But Ann's enthusiasm is infectious. She really knows how to cut loose.

The picnic tables are literally covered with dishes and trays of food. Dad delivers foil packets from the fire. We don't know exactly what roasted things we'll find in them. Things get quiet as we settle in for some serious feasting. The grown-ups congregate around the campsite and most of us kids sit together on the beach. We tell stories and tease one another and eat. Mom put slices of onion in with the perch that got roasted on the fire, and it's burned a little around the edges, giving the fish a sweet smoky caramelized flavor. This is heaven on a plate. None of us saves room for dessert, but nonetheless we all have dessert. A heaping serving of Auntie's blueberry cobbler and one of Barb's strawberry shortcake. Maybe two. Homemade baking soda biscuits sliced in half like a cookie and filled with sliced strawberries, with a big dollop of whip cream on top, the real thing, naturally. No telling how it got whipped. This must have been Barb's deal and mom probably stayed out of it. She did know when she was outgunned.

After dessert, we all moan and groan, our bellies straining, but we are happy. We sit around the campfire and tell stories and sing. Dancing light flickers on faces, old and young, we gaze into the fire, we may reflect for moments on what's deep within. There's a bed of glowing red coals under the flames, into which we ease empty beer bottles closer and closer gradually heating them, and then into the coals they go. We watch them turn red and get soft and sag and melt into odd organic blobs, prizes to be dug out in the morning.

And morning comes, promising another hot and humid New Hampshire summer day. We're all stumbling around in our morning grogginess, mom and dad are probably suffering the after effects of too much to drink, and the Texas Contingent rolls in. They're all bright and perky and showered and trim and smell good. How they do this is a mystery. Mom and Aunt Ann again do the work that never ends, they hustle up more coffee and make breakfast. First, a mountain of bacon and then blueberry pancakes. I watch the goings-on and mom grins and asks me, "Plain pancakes for you?"

"I'll pass on blueberries, if it means I don't have to pick them," I say.

Mom knows I just hate picking the darn things and says, "It's O.K. We'll make blueberry pancakes for you too." Mom has two round cast iron griddles squeezed on top of the camp stove. They're seasoned from years of use and careful cleaning. She puts vegetable oil on them and when they begin to smoke, ladles on pancake batter filled with blueberries. The small round cakes sputter and start to bubble through, she gives them another minute and turns them, splat, splat, splat! The berries hiss when they hit the hot griddle, and in another moment they're ready to go, each cake golden brown with little spots of hot blueberry juice bleeding through. She keeps both griddles going, and as quickly as the cakes appear on plates, they vanish. And on it goes, mom cooks, we devour. Slather on plenty of butter and pour on the maple syrup. And this is Maple Syrup, the stuff that comes from trees, the real deal. The flavors, the tart-sweet of wild blueberries, the richness of the syrup and butter... About two and a half plates full of pancakes later, again, I am stuffed.

As the day heats up, Vic stretches out on a folding chaise lounge on the beach by the shuffleboard court. Inspired by the Texans, she's working on her tan. Actually she's working on her sunburn / peel cycle, but oh, if only we could get it right and end up with that beautiful, coveted bronze glow. She's laying there on her stomach, in her bathing suit, peaceful, maybe half snoozing. And of course this is all just way too peaceful for me to allow it to continue. I saunter over to say hello.

"Hi Vic," I say.

Vic opens one eye and glances at me warily. "Hi Nodrog," she says. "What's going on?" Nodrog is one of my nicknames, the full version is Nodrog Reknub.

"Not much. Just here to say hello." I sit down in the sand beside her. Vic keeps an eye on me, and for good reason. But this time I just hang out. It really seems I'm here just to hang out. Vic relaxes. "It's hot today," I say.

"No kidding," says Vic, her voice muffled by the towel she's got rolled up for a pillow. She peeks at me, just to be sure I'm not up to something. This is when I crane my neck a little, then some more, looking at her back. "What?" asks Vic, the slightest edge of concern has crept into her voice. Slowly I sit up to get a better look. "What?" she asks again, now with genuine agitation.

"Vic," I say. Her body tenses. "Don't move."

"What is it?!?" she asks, alarmed.

"Hold still!" I say. "There's a spider on your back. On your bathing suit." Vic's body exudes tension. She flinches.

"No! Don't move!" I say.

"What color is it?!?" she asks.

"Black," I say.

"Is it shiny?!?" she asks.

"Yes," I say, and motion to get up. "I'll kill it."

"NO!" exclaims Vic, who remains motionless as a stone. "You miss it, and it's gonna bite me!"

I sit back and look at Vic. "I'll get mom," I say. "She'll know what to do."

"O.K., but hurry!" says Vic. I get up and run to the tent.

Of course there is no spider, there never was any spider, and I do not go back. I can see Vic laying there, petrified, in a state of motionless frenzy. A few minutes later she yells in the general direction of the tent, "Nodrog!" I take my time and walk half way to her. "Where's mom?!?" I shrug my shoulders. "Is the spider still there?!?" she asks.

I peer toward her, pause, and shrug my shoulders again. Vic lifts her head up. "Nodrog! Was there *ever* a spider???"

"Nope," I say. And I take off at a run, and Vic jumps up and comes after me.

"I AM GOING TO KILL YOU!!!" she screams, and chases me all over the place. Panting for breath, I get on the other side of the Buick and she tries unsuccessfully, to get me, until Uncle

Mike sneaks up from behind and grabs me. I scream and wiggle and try to get loose but to no avail. He's a lot bigger than me. Vic comes stomping around the car.

"I all caught me this *varmint*," says Uncle Mike. "Yawl interested to... tickle him while I hold on?"

Vic comes at me, fire in her eyes, looking forward to this, and lets me have it. And I deserve it.

While the Texans are visiting we also have a cookout at Barb and Pamp's. This means exposure to the dreaded aspic salad, but in small quantities I'm getting used to it. Barb and Pamp live in the caretaker's cottage across the road from the estate they look after. It's a neat little place on a hill with grey cedar shingle siding and yellow trim. The main house is on a point of land with sweeping views of the lake. Pamp takes us over for a look. A long driveway winds its way through manicured lawns and trees, the setting is serene. The house has a porch wrapped around it, comfortable looking wicker furniture with big cushions is set out, but no one's there. We step out on the dock. The air is soft, full to the brim with moisture, and waves splash on the granite bouldered shore. Giant inboard speedboats thunder by at high speeds, well kept people in them with their hair swept back smile and laugh and wave. This is my first exposure to big money. It's all so very odd, so controlled, so out of touch. The wildness is gone. But it is very attractive and perhaps this is what it's all about.

The best part of visiting Barb and Pamp is sneaking through the woods to the Goodhue & Hawkins Navy Yard, typically during the long summer evenings after the place is closed. All the day's hustle and bustle is over, everyone has gone home and it's quiet. They haven't thought of fencing the place off, or a security guard, so I wander around the place, exploring the old storage barns. They are shady and filled with cool damp lake air and the old boats. I can hear waves on shore and the exhausts of speedboats thundering by. In the early 1900's Goodhue & Hawkins built boats in a distinctive style known as "Lakers." These are long and narrow displacement hulls with plumb stems, plenty of bow flare and sides sweeping back to the stern with generous tumblehome. They are designed to cut though the waves and give a smooth ride, a number of these old timers sit on cradles in the barns. A boat in the water is a dynamic thing, in constant motion, even when tied to a dock. But here on the cradles they are still. I study their lines. The big hulls loom above me, ghostly. Climbing up on the cradles, I can see into the cockpits. Seats are upholstered in tufted leather, in dark reds and greens. Hardware and trim are polished bronze or nickel plated. Beautiful wood rimmed steering wheels on polished bronze hubs. Chocks and cleats, navigation lights, spotlights with prismatic lenses. All so quiet, sitting and waiting. Waiting for their time again, on the water.

Birds nest in the rafters, they are coming home for the night, they chirp and flutter about. They line up and have their little conversations, wondering what's going on with this intruder.

And there are engines, great cast iron monstrosities, much bigger than anything found in cars. They too are dynamic things, although much of their movement is internal and unseen. They create the dynamism, they power the great boats hurtling through the water, leaving a wake and spray and bellowing exhaust notes. Here, they are quiet and still. Sleeping. Waiting. These barns are mysterious and magical places. My appreciation grows for these old wooden boats.

We get home late enough that we all wash up and go directly to bed. Keeping the bottom of the door unzipped for

Tippy has worked well. He can come and go as he wants. Given he sleeps most of every day, the night time must be the right time for his own set of summertime adventures. In the middle of the night, it is pitch black dark. The only outdoor lighting in the entire campground is a lone bulb hanging outside the bath house, and the bug zappers. So who knows what time it is, or which way is up. From the nighttime stillness and calm suddenly there is a commotion at the unzipped door and before we know what's going on a cat fight explodes into the tent... and then on top of mom in her sleeping bag.

Screeching! Screaming! Howling! Spitting! Mom shouting! It is complete, utter, chaos! Worse than anything mom and Auntie get into. Vic and I wake up, "Mom? Are you ok?" we call into the darkness... "What's going on?"

"Argh! Eeek!" says mom. A flashlight snaps on.

More screeching clawing and spitting. Two hairy blurs have each other in a death grip at the foot of her sleeping bag. Chunks of fur fly in the air. Low howling. Mom rolls up a magazine and swats them. "O.K. you two! Get out of here!" she yells. She swats them again. And they break it up and the pumpkin intruder makes a run for it and Tippy goes after him. The two cats vanish under the door.

Mom's sitting up and unzips her sleeping bag. She has a big gash in her calf muscle that's bleeding at a good clip. "Damn it all!" she says.

"Mom are you O.K.?" we ask. "Do you need to go to the hospital?"

Mom gets up, the dim beam of her flashlight wiggles around the tent. "I'll be O.K. Just let me wash this up..." Things settle down and when she's through cleaning the wound, she zips the bottom of the door shut. "Let the damn cat stay outside and think about it," she mutters. After all the commotion we go back to sleep.

The next morning dad gets up first. He's puzzled by the door being zippered. He looks around, "Why's the zipper… what's all this cat hair doing in here?" he asks.

Mom props herself up. "You didn't hear the cat fight?" she asks.

"What cat fight?" asks dad, groggy and clueless.

Mom is incredulous. "You didn't hear it?!? The kids woke up…!" she stammers.

"No…" says dad, sheepishly. He yawns.

We tell him the story. Mom sits there fuming. "What if it had been a tiger and it ate me?" she asks.

Dad scratches his head and thinks about this for a minute. He says, "Well, I'd miss you."

"You'd miss me?" asks mom. "That's it?"

"Yep," says dad, master of understatement. "I need to go to the boys room."

Mom gets up. "He would have missed me. I can't believe it." she mutters under her breath. "He'd miss me." She starts making coffee. When dad gets back from the boys room she glowers at him. "*You* can make breakfast this morning," she says.

"What did I do?" he asks.

"Nothing!" says mom.

We end up having cold cereal from the little individual boxes. To dress them up dad offers slices of banana.

. . .

Nearing the end of another 180 day sentence, a big thick envelope with exotic stamps and stickers on it arrives from the Nova Scotia Department of Tourism. And one evening right about then, dad comes home from work with a brochure on Nimrod pop-up camper trailers. Times, they are a changing.

We sit around the kitchen table together and peruse through what the folks in Nova Scotia sent. Pictures of beautiful sweeping lush green landscapes and miles of pristine beaches, blue ocean and clear air, quaint fishing villages, boats moored in harbors, peace and quiet, and big plates of the freshest seafood at every stop. Sprinkle in a few bonne redhead lasses and some manly men in kilts for mom and Vic, and bingo, decision made. We're going to Nova Scotia!

And then we have the material on Nimrod campers. These little babies are low profile and light weight. They tow like a breeze, you'll hardly know it's hitched onto your car. This will turn out to be true, given the Buick's 38:1 weight advantage. Maybe I'm exaggerating. It's probably more like 42:1. (kidding) But of course there are pictures of happy campers in lovely settings. It's easy to put the two together; explore the Maritime Provinces... with the pop-up camper. Voila!

Never do you see dog bites, bee stings, drunkenness, hangovers, spontaneous projectile throw up, menstrual cramps, fog, swarms of blood sucking insects, arguments, getting lost, torrential rain, thunder, lightning, running out of gas, flat tires, overheating engines, overheating brakes, or boredom. Not once. Marketing people are just so clever and the rest of us are just so optimistic. We want to believe the lofty claims of the brochures and so we do, and we do the reasonable thing. We buy the pop-up camper and schedule a service for the new(er) Buick at Simard's Esso.

Sadly, along the way the old green Buick died a slow corrosive death. The last straw was when mom got in the car one afternoon wearing heels and put one of them through the floor, and adding insult to injury, the shoe got stuck there. So the Ol' 225 with all its glorious swoopiness still intact went to the glue factory and a newer, considerably bigger, boxier and thus bland Buick Electra 225 *Limited* (to two million copies, plus or minus) took its place.

Mom and dad are getting to a point where sleeping on cots has lost its charm. Actually, sleeping on cots never had any charm. Unless you think back pain is charming. The tent is getting tired, it is a bear to pitch and take down, and it weighs a ton. And for traveling, towing a trailer means we increase the space available for all the junk we want to bring along. Cool. Done!

Dad and I get in the Buick one Saturday morning to go to Haggett's and get the trailer, and being in such close proximity to Louis' Diner, we first stop for coffee and donuts. Properly sweetened and caffeinated we head for the shop and there's Dana, smiling. The guys install a trailer hitch on the car and fiddle with the wiring and soon we're driving home with the trailer in tow. I keep looking back and yep, it's still there, happily bobbing along. The white vinyl top has ballooned up in the wind, like a giant marshmallow.

Whoever dreamed up the original pop-up camper is a genius. After the original, like everything else in the U.S. of A., new and improved just means bigger and more complicated and heavier, and sadly pop-up campers are not exempt. The little Nimrod however, is a gem. We get it home, and discover a feature not mentioned in the brochure: a short wheelbase. This makes backing the thing up very tricky. Backing up any trailer is tricky, but the shorter the wheelbase the quicker the trailer will jackknife on you.

So dad struggles with this and mom comes out. She is all excited, and starts giving directions, or as dad would suggest starts telling him what to do. I sit on the breezeway and keep out of it. Vic comes out and sits down beside me. She asks, "What are they doing?"

"Their best not to get into a fight," I answer.

With the help of mom's shouting and wild gesticulations, dad gets the trailer backed into the driveway. It's plain to see he would have rather not had the "help," but he cuts mom some slack. She's excited, which is great to see.

And now it's time to set it up. Oh boy. Even more fun. The first time it takes us two hours to figure out. With experience we eventually get this down to fifteen minutes, maybe even less depending on how hard it's raining. Folding jacks at each corner of the trailer swing down, lock into place and telescope out to meet the ground for support. Unsnap and remove the white vinyl cover. Unlatch and pull out the two opposing beds and the tent starts its way up. Then fiddle with extending a few poles, and snap a few snaps and there she is! Just like that, home away from home. Dad stands back and sticks out his stomach. "Where's the beer?" he asks.

The trailer has neat wood grain decals on the sides, looks just like, well, almost like mahogany, and a little hinged door with a latch that locks. Dad opens the door and unzips the front zipper and sweeps his hand over the threshold, bows and says to mom, "After you, madam."

And mom steps into the trailer. She stands there for a moment and looks around, then dad and I and Vic get in. Wow, this is cool. It's still, sort of, a tent, but the beds are cushy and it has a floor. Tippy hops in. He looks around and gives it a sniff and in his classic nonplussed cat way, leaves.

"That cat doesn't know high class accommodations when he sees them," says dad. We sit on the edges of the beds and look at each other. Now what?

Mom has plans, which means plans for dad which for dad means another project. And this in turn means plans for me, but I'm cool. It will be some guy time with dad and I'm always into that. The plan is to build two benches, a dining table and a table for the three, count 'em *three* burner stove mom has picked out at Sears. We are gonna be stylin'!

Dad and I set about building the cabinets and tables. The design envelope doesn't include anything about fine cherry wood craftsmanship, instead we're talking cobbled together and functional. What dad may lack in woodworking skills he makes up with drafting skills. He comes up with a set of beautiful pencil drawings with dimensions and notes with squiggly arrows denoting where this or that detail is relevant. And there are goofy little cartoon faces peeking around corners and edges.

Knowing full well there is no such thing as one trip to the hardware store we embark on this adventure in construction. With a list of materials in hand, we first go to Concord Lumber for 2x4's and plywood and imitation walnut grain paneling. The finished product may not be fine, but it will have class. Albeit imitation class. And we'll go to Wilber's Hardware for all the little bits and pieces; nails, screws, L-brackets, and hinges and latches with fake brass plating. Concord Lumber and Wilber's, after the aquarium shop, are two of my favorite places. They are places where the men - and about one woman every three years - who build things go. We have ideas in our minds, pencils behind our ears and tape measures clipped to our belts. And lists of materials on clipboards. The smells of spicy pine and pungent oak fill the air at the lumber yard, along with whines and rips of powerful saws cutting lengths and widths to order. Shiny tools of the trade are on display, all with ancient heritage; squares, levels, plumb bobs. Chalk lines, saws and hammers of all description. I wander around the store while dad orders the lumber. The clerk produces a ticket which we will take around to the yard where surly guys will help us gather it all up and lash it down, somehow, to the car. From their perspective, we're the weekend warriors who don't know diddly-squat about what we're doing and are largely pains in their behinds. Saturday mornings, they deal with too many customers who think they'll just throw a half dozen sheets of plywood on the top of the car and drive out of there holding it down with their hands, raised up through open windows. Yeah, right. We at least have the roof rack on the Peug, and some decent lengths of rope, so we command some small modicum of respect from the crew. With their manly help we lash our goodies onto the rack and head for Wilber's.

Clyde Wilber is a guy who loves his job. He's wiry and high energy and bald and wears bifocals. Or maybe trifocals. He greets us like long lost friends and knows where *everything* is in the store. And I do mean every thing. No. 8 x 32 nuts, brass, you need six of them? Right over here. Half inch lamp wick? Just around the corner. A quart of #744 Prussian blue oil base (for something mom's up to), satin? Let's get that mixed while we're finding your nuts. So to speak. #6 ring nails with a walnut finish? How many pounds? Sixteen L-brackets, twelve L-plates, a half pound of #8 x 1½ wood screws, do you want slotted or Phillips head? Eight surface mount cabinet hinges, four door catches, brass finish with screws. The quart of paint flails wildly on the mixer. We loiter with Mr. Wilber while the paint continues to shake.

He smiles and looks at dad. "So how you been?" he asks. "How's Elna?"

Dad looks at him, bewildered, our heads are spinning from the romp around the store. "Fine," dad shouts, "yeah, just fine." And when the paint stops shaking, Mr. Wilber very authoritatively releases the big screw clamps that hold onto the can, puts the can on the counter, opens it. "Yep, 744 Prussian," he says. He dips his finger in the paint and puts a dab on the outside of the cover, puts the cover on the can and then puts the can in his special paint can closing machine, gives it a squeeze and immensely satisfied with everything, hands it to dad and says, "Bunk, thanks so much, and hello to the missus." And in a flash, he's off to the next customer. The whole visit, soup to nuts takes ten minutes. We leave, happy and dazed.

We're in the wrong end of town for coffee and donuts at Louis', but Garbo's is right across the street and we stop there for hot roast beef sandwiches on onion rolls. And they're not shy with the onions. I think the Garbo family is from Sicily, the guys who work there are all big and round and dark and have their hair slicked back, and they know how to roast a beef and put a sandwich together. And make pizza and grinders. We walk in and one of the guy shouts at us, "Wa u wan!?!" We order four sandwiches to go and he nods. Given the difference in our language skills, it amazes me he gets it, but he does. Growing up I always had a thing for these sandwiches, which may explain why most of the girls I talked to basically wilted and wanted to get away. Or at the very least, up wind.

We bring our booty home, have lunch and get to work. Dad's left the Peug outside. We set up sawhorses in his side of the garage and bring the materials in, setting the 2x4's on the horses and leaning the plywood and paneling up against the wall. We tackle the first order of business and build the frames. This takes us the rest of the day, and what we end up with while not pretty is plenty sturdy, and we're happy. The next day we cut and attach the walnut grain paneling, using the little walnut color nails. Over the following week we futz with the cabinet doors and hardware. In the mean time, dad goes to the plumbing supply and has lengths of iron pipe cut and threaded for table legs, and threaded pipe flanges to attach them to the undersides of the tables. We make trip #2 to Wilber's for crutch tips for the bottom ends of the legs. The idea is, everything needs to be stowed in the trailer under the sliding beds, so the cabinets can be no more than a certain height and the tables need to be easily broken down.

Mom and Vic have been making an upholstered cushion for the dining bench and they've picked out some colorful oilcloth to cover the tabletops. It all works pretty well when we get it finished and together. The tables, on their pipe legs are a bit wobbly, but as dad says, "What do you want... an egg in your beer?" We're all pleased with our accomplishments, and now ready to hit the road.

The plan is to spend the summer at Robie's as usual, but now, when dad takes his 2 week vacation we can easily break camp to go exploring... and this summer it will be Nova Scotia.

Once again thank goodness, like the rising and setting of the sun, like the turn of the seasons, Vic's and my time in school comes to an end, we take off our shoes, pack it up and head for the lake. This year it all takes on a distinct wagon train effect, with the new XL Buick and the addition of the trailer. So now it's a behemoth, the trailer and the little Peug behind, with Starcraft frosting on top. We make quite a scene going down the road.

In an effort to stop or at least reduce the howling and whistling and moaning the roof racks make, dad has stuffed foam into the open channels of the cross beams, and wrapped them with tape. As soon as we set out we find it is all for naught. So mom and Vic and Tippy enjoy the relative cool and calm of the Buick and dad and I, once again do our best to stay sane in the mobile chamber of aural horrors.

It takes us a while to work the bugs out of our new setup, but right away there are clear advantages with the pop-up camper. For example, when it pours rain all night, the floor doesn't flood. It's all so new and spacious and comfy, and perhaps its greatest feature is in having a zippered entry. There are few sounds that say, "welcome home" more than a tent zipper being zipped. And we still have the comforting sounds of rain drops hitting the canvas, I relax and get sleepy just thinking about these sounds. We've also set up a folding table outside, right by the door and left the snaps between the canvas and the body of the trailer undone, so Tippy can nose his way in and out. Watching his head appear in the gap, especially when he looks around and decides he'd rather stay out, and slip, out goes his head, is pretty funny. Pop goes the weasel, or the cat as it were.

On breezy hot days, with all the screens open, I enjoy sprawling out on top of my sleeping bag next to the end window to read. With an elevated view of the woods, it becomes my favorite, private little nook. With the soft air coming in from the lake, as often as not I end up taking a nap.

We easily fall into our summer routines, but all of us have Canada on our minds. The big envelope of tourist information is now well used, and every day one or more of us takes a brochure or map to study and dream over. The Maritime Provinces seem so exotic, so far away, in another country, no less. In about a month we'll pack it up and take off for two weeks.

Making preparations to leave Robies in the middle of summer feels so odd, and Tippy knows something's up. We pull the boat up on shore, remove the engine and turn it upside down, and we take Tippy to the cat kennel, poor creature. And in the dim light of a July dawn we fold up the camper and hit the road. We'll be all day heading north and east across Maine and by nightfall we cross the border in Saint Stephen, New Brunswick.

I love Canada, starting with the flag. Choosing a maple leaf as your national symbol, celebrating a love of nature and environment, how cool is that? The young woman at customs is as friendly as she can be, asking dad a few questions and wishing us a fine stay in her country. We find our way through Saint Stephen - it's a quiet mill town on the St. Croix River that's seen better times. After a full day and part of a night on the road, we spend our first night in Canada in a mom & pop motel. There's a make do approach to things here, and people are friendlier than at home.

The next morning we have a simple breakfast from the cooler, cold cereal with milk and fruit. Mom has strategically placed the cooler and things we'll need for breakfasts and lunches on the road right inside the camper door. Of course there's always one thing or another that's a reach to get to...

Dad is the family photographer. He's got the Kodak 35 and the light meter, and is snapping a few pictures for the record. Mom's got her head stuck in the trailer, looking for paper plates and her butt is sticking out. Dad can't resist. He takes the first of what will be many pictures of mom's butt sticking out of that door. "Here's mom's butt sticking out in Saint Stephen... Here's mom's butt sticking out on the Gaspe Peninsula! Beautiful country isn't it? Here's mom's butt sticking out in front of The Canadian Parliament Building."

When we get to St. John, nothing will do but to check out the reversing falls on the St. John River. "It looks like a river," I say.

"You see the rapids and the water flowing out?" asks dad.

"Yep," I say.

"Just wait," says dad. We're now on the shore of The Bay of Fundy, a place known for extreme tides, at times up to fifty vertical feet of water. We're all perched on a bluff, overlooking the river. "Pretty soon the water will go the other way."

We sit there for a long, long time. "It still looks like a river," I say. "Can we go now?"

"Just sit tight," says dad. "How about I get a picture of you and your sister?"

"O.K.," I say, but I'm not really into it. Nonetheless Vic and I stand there on the bluff overlooking the so-called reversing falls and dad takes our picture. I'm beginning to wonder whether

181

or not this family road trip thing is such a good idea. Dad turns his attention to the river.

"Look, it's reversing," he says, and sure enough, the rapids have gone slack. So we wait for another eternity, and as advertised, the water goes the other way. The tide comes in, the flow in the river goes upstream.

"So what?" I ask. Reflecting on this, the word brat comes to mind. Dad tries to explain what's going on with the water. He seems to be impressed. "Can we go *now*?" I ask. And he shoots me a look like I'm on the verge of getting in trouble and I just look at him and grin.

When we first get to Nova Scotia, we spend some time exploring the little town of Truro, and check out the bore tide on the Shubenacadie (say this one three times fast) River. We pull off to the side of the road and get out of the car at a place overlooking a broad and stinky mud flat with a little trickle of water running through it. "Looks like a mud flat to me," I say.

"Listen buster, just hold onto your shorts," says dad, this time cutting me no slack.

So I do my best to loiter and not cause trouble. Which is a tall order. And we wait. For a long time and dad has the camera out and is taking pictures. Pictures of a mud flat. Woo-hoo! Can't wait until the family slide shows for this one. "Our trip to Nova Scotia… here's a picture of a mud flat!" And Auntie Tora will look at this one and lean over to mom and say, "That Bunk sure knows how to take a picture…"

But sure enough, here comes a wave of water roaring its way *up* the river, and it goes rushing on by and the river is full of water. Just like that. Dad is snapping pictures for the before and after effect. O.K., I got to admit, this one is impressive. "That's cool," I say. Dad looks at me and winks.

We notice there's less wealth in the Maritime Provinces. Towns are small and buildings, for the most part, lack any kind of fanciness. But we also notice Canadians have a greater sense of pride. Not in a flag waving way, but in how they live. Passing through little fishing villages in Nova Scotia, even the smallest and plainest of houses is neat as a pin. No junk cars, no sheds falling in on themselves. It's a pleasant change from U.S.A.

We make it as far north as Cape Breton Island. With an influx of folks from Scotland, a thick brogue is spoken and everyone, well, not quite *everyone*, wears skirts. "Dad, the men here wear skirts," I say, not knowing quite what to make of this.

"Those are kilts, not skirts," dad tells me, "and those guys wearing them tend to take it pretty seriously, so don't make any wise comments, O.K.?"

I can't help but add, "They look like skirts to me." At one of the places we stop there are a bunch of guys milling around, all of them wearing skir... kilts. They're forming up to play the bagpipes, they've got their hands full with these gangly, honking, wheezing things. When they get it together and start to play "Amazing Grace," dad stands there quietly, with his eyes closed and tears stream down his face. Seeing him so moved, we all join in, the four of us stand there and cry. Dad, and so Vic and I have some Scot in us. Just why I don't know, but since then whenever I hear the pipes, the music touches me very, very deeply. There's something about the pipes, the sounds are in our blood.

Heading around the far reaches of the island we drive the Cabot Trail, a rollercoaster of a road following the shore. With the car loaded down and towing the trailer, the engine overheats going up the hills and brakes overheat going down. So we stop a lot and dad takes pictures. We have a lot of pictures from scenic overlooks, beautiful green hills, and blue ocean stretching out forever. And a few of course, of mom's butt.

It's time to start heading home. Dad's vacation time is coming to a close, and we have the rest of the summer on the lake to look forward to. We put on the miles and our last night in Canada, somewhere in New Brunswick, we pull into a campground way up on a hill, in a dense fog, in the night. It all seems nice enough, we'll only spend the night and we're all tired. We get the camper set up and hit the sack.

And... CRASH!

What was that!?!

BOOM! and CRASH!... and... another BOOM!

"I think your mother dropped her teeth," says dad, and for some reason, maybe that she has dentures, mom doesn't find this particularly funny. The rest of us try our best to squelch the giggles. CRASH!... We look at one another. What the heck is going on? But it seems we're all safe and snug, so it's lights BOOM! out. The ruckus goes on all night, and none of us is able to sleep.

Next morning CRASH!, the sun comes up, we stir in our sleeping bags, and bleary-eyed, stumble BOOM! out of bed. None of is even remotely perky, but we are curious to know what's been going on. Once out of the trailer, we discover our campsite is literally on the very edge of a steep precipice with a two hundred or so foot drop to a rail yard. Welcome to the great outdoors! Savor the wilderness experience! We all look at one another and shake our CRASH! heads.

When we get home, Tippy is some kind of glad to see us and we're glad to see him. And it's good to settle in to life back at the lake.

. . .

A summer or two later, Vic has a job at The Brook and Bridle Inn, and is living in one of the dormitories the inn has for the staff. Can you say, "*Party?*" It's a big change for all of us, Vic being gone and on her own. Our mobile adventures take us to Maine, this time waay into the back woods...

Dad is buddies with Walker Pierce from Air Force days. They were parts of a crew together, and Walker is a good natured and quick witted wild man. He sells cars at the local Chevrolet dealership in Portland, Maine. Our families get together from time to time for weekend visits, and Walker and his wife Joan have a daughter, Patricia. Her dad nicknamed her Laughing Loon, and without delay we all adopt this name for her.

The Pierce's have mentioned their summer camp on Moosehead Lake, and invite us to go there with them for a week. We all have a fun time when we get together so we take them up on it. We stock the liquor cabinet, pack extra warm clothing and put in a good supply of bug repellant. This is about all you really need to survive a week in the back woods of Maine. The state bird in these parts is the black fly. Get back into the boonies and you'll encounter clouds of them that given half a chance will carry you away, and Moosehead Lake is definitely back in the boonies.

We spend a night with the Pierce's at their house and bright and early the next morning it's wheels up and we're off into the woods. It takes all day to get to the lake, the last fifty or so miles is hammering along on dirt roads. Walker has a hot rod Impala, it has the biggest engine in it Chevy offers and he likes to put his foot in it. The Buick is no match, especially towing the trailer, but Walker is patient. We're taking a break at a pull-out, basically swatting black flies and thinking why don't we just get back into the cars and go when dad points at the front of Walker's car. What? Did he hit a bear and just not notice?

Dad starts snickering. "*Walker, what are these?*" he asks.

Walker grins. He knows what dad's looking at. It turns out he put aircraft landing lights in the high beam sockets of the Impala. "They light up the road pretty good," he says, and laughs.

"I'll bet!" says dad.

"Watch this," says Walker. He starts the Chevy, turns on the lights and flicks on the high beams. The engine nearly stalls under the load. The lamps are dazzlingly bright. I hold my hand in front of one, but only for a second, the heat is that intense. My hand glows bright red, as though I were holding it up to the sun.

"Good for jackin' deer," says mom to Walker on the sly.

"Don't you know it, " says Walker.

The roads get narrower and rougher the further into the woods we go, until by the end of it, Walker unlocks a chain draped from two rusty iron pipes across a pair of mud pocked ruts and we hump and bump the final half mile to the "camp." Turns out the building is a recycled barrack Walker absconded from the military. It's easy to see why the government gave it up, yep, country livin' at its finest. It is a shack to which a gallon of

186

gasoline and a match would do a big favor. This might be an exaggeration, but might not. As soon as we get out of our cars, the bugs descend on us. We quickly douse ourselves with bug juice, which keeps all but the most determined at bay. Which is another way of saying we're getting bit a lot. But we take a moment to survey the scene and see we are on the shore of one of the most beautiful lakes in the world.

Moosehead is a glacial lake, about 40 by 10 miles with some 80 islands in it, and because of its remoteness, there are only a handful of camps around it. Looking out across the water, it's a rarity to see a boat, and at night it's dark. It is a remarkable place, a place of unspoiled beauty.

There's a rough clearing between the cottage and lake. We manage to get the trailer situated without getting the car stuck - when it comes time to haul the trailer out it may be a different story - and get the top popped up, and it rains. We all scramble for cover. A half hour or so later, Joan comes down to the trailer in her yellow rain slicker. We unzip the front door and she pokes her head in. "You all ok in here?" she asks, bless her heart. We respond in the affirmative. "Whenever you like, come on up," she offers. "Might be nice to be under a roof for a while." And seeing how it's the cocktail hour, this sounds like a pretty good idea, so we put on our slickahs and walk up to the camp.

We make our entrance and drape our soaking jackets on the backs of chairs. The Pierce's are full of smiles and good cheer. "Welcome to our modest country abode," says Walker. This is when we notice they have buckets and pots and wash basins set all over the place catching water as it pours through the roof.

Mom laughs. "*Our* roof doesn't leak," she teases.

"The home improvement committee has plans to rectify this situation," says Walker. "Don't you worry, little lady."

If there's one way to get mom's goat, it's to call her, at all of five foot one, "little lady." Mom shoots Walker a look, like watch it, Bub. And so the evening begins... Laughing Loon and I retreat to play go fish and checkers.

Mom decides she needs to use the privy. Walker gets up from his chair, "Hold on a second, Elna," he says, and he gets a small box. "Here, you might need this," he says. Mom opens the box. She pulls out a dried corn cob that has an electrical cord coming out of one end. The grown-ups all roar with laughter. Laughing Loon and I just look at one another not having a clue. Grown-ups find humor in the strangest things.

"What's so funny about that?" I ask.

Mom in her hysteria wheezes, tries her best to explain between guffaws, "Way back in the olden days... people in the back woods didn't have toilet paper. So they'd use dried corn cobs..." She's holding on to the thing, the cord dangles down, and the joke is doubly funny in that there's no source of electricity for 50 miles. The corn cob got hung on a special cup hook in the outhouse.

When mom gets back she quips, "There's no door on the outhouse!" She looks at Walker. "The least you could do..."

"Wouldn't want to spoil the view of the lake," says Walker. He does have a point. I'd never used a toilet with such a view. Kind of peaceful and relaxing to look at while you sit there. "But there are ladies present, so..." Walker ponders a solution, after all he wants the ladies to be comfortable.

"I have just the thing," says mom. "Don't worry about it."

Water continues to pour through the roof and when one of the buckets fills Walker grabs it, runs to the door and tosses the contents outside, then rushes back to catch the torrent. It's getting on toward supper time and we decide to move the party to the camper.

It's cozy in the camper with six of us squeezed in there. The Coleman lantern takes the chill and some of the dampness out of the air, and mom and Joan cook up a giant pot full of spaghetti, with homemade sauce mom brought from what she had in the freezer back home. We have little shakers of oregano, red pepper and grated cheese, and we have a feast and party late into the rainy night. I go out to water a tree, it is dark, really dark outside. Looking back at the camper, the canvas is all aglow, I can hear voices and laughter, a small spot of warmth and good cheer in these vast, dark and quiet woods.

Next morning after coffee, mom's on her hands and knees digging around in one of the cabinets, dad's sitting there wishing he had the camera, and mom pulls out a shower curtain, decorated with bright color tropical fish, no less. My mother never ceases to amaze me... *why* she would bring a shower curtain is one of those mysteries, but she did. She also has a supply of thumb tacks, so with these she walks through the weeds over to the privy and tacks up the curtain over the doorway. So now, standing in a clearing in the wilderness is an outhouse with a tropical fish shower curtain door. And an electric corn cob dangling from a cup hook. The funny thing is, somehow it all makes perfect sense. Everyone is appreciative of this homey finishing touch.

The sun is out and it's a glorious day. Laughing Loon and I go out in the row boat, our folks make it clear we are not to go too far. There's 40 miles of water out there in which it might not take too much effort to get lost. So we stay within sight of the dock. The water is calm and a half dozen or so loons are swimming about.

"Stop rowing for a minute," says Laughing Loon. I bring the oars inside the boat and we drift. All is quiet. The loons dive, swim underwater, sometimes for great distances, and then pop up. Laughing Loon slowly rises to her feet. She takes in a big gulp of air, tips her head back and calls out, "AH-Loooo-oooo-oo!" I sit there, flabbergasted, that such a great and haunting song can come from such a little kid. I've never heard anything like it, except from a loon. She calls again, "AH-Loooo-ooo!" And darned if the loons don't call back. She looks at me, all excited, and giggles and grins. "How about that?" I don't know what to say. And the loons call her and she calls back, and they have a wonderful sing-along chat.

There will be times around camp we will hear loons calling from the water and as often as not one of the voices will be Laughing Loon, standing by herself on the end of the dock, singing her heart out.

In the mean time, a red squirrel has positioned itself in a tree between the outhouse and our camper and it is chattering incessantly. On and on and on and... I do mean incessantly. And we throw stones at it, shout, wave our arms, don't go away mad, just go away! But all our efforts and it doesn't budge an inch. Or keep quiet. Mom has had enough. Walker is sunning himself on the front porch of the camp, and taking it all in. Mom shouts up to him, "Walker, we've come all the way up here for some peace and quiet!" she rants, standing there with hands on hips. "Aren't you going to do *something* about this racket?!?"

190

Walker gets up and goes inside the camp. In a moment he reappears, holding an ungodly large caliber big game rifle. Standing there in just a bathing suit and flip-flops he raises the rifle, takes aim and KA-POW!, shoots the squirrel. What little is left of it falls from the tree, *splat!*, right smack dab on top of our camper. Walker quietly goes back in the camp and puts the rifle away. He comes back out and sits down in his lawn chair as though this is just another day of protecting his tribe from wild animals in the deep woods of Maine.

"Takes care of that," says Walker. I stand there, mouth agape. You can now hear a pin drop. No more chatter from the squirrel, or mom. And it's not often mom is at a loss for something smart to say.

"Thank you Walker," says mom, primly. She gets a stick and removes the squirrel's remains from the tent and then rinses most of the blood off with a bucket or two of lake water. But there are stains in the camper top, a reminder which will be there for the rest of its days.

We've enjoyed a couple days of fair weather, but it's looking like rain is coming in from the southeast. Walker probably can't face the notion of reprimands coming from all quarters as they did the last time the roof was leaking, so he and dad join forces to do some home improvements. Time for a little honey dew, so to speak. Walker has a supply of boards and nails, and a few rolls of asphalt roofing, they should have things snug as a bug in no time. But there's some drinking going on…

They get an extension ladder, and a step ladder and get to work, peeling off the old roofing and replacing rotten boards and this and that and are having a jolly time, the two of them like overgrown boy-scouts in their bathing suits and flip flops. They're swatting bugs and making comments and laughing, and actually getting the job done. Things are looking pretty good. Joan and mom look on approvingly and give moral support. Knowing mom, she might also be telling them how to do it.

I decide to stay clear of this enterprise, but can't help my curiosity when I hear the chain saw. Home improvements and chainsaws are an unusual combination, one that sounds like trouble. Laughing Loon and I join the audience. Rough ends of boards jut out from the eave of the camp in all odd lengths. Walker is standing on the top of the step ladder with the running chainsaw over his head. He's going to trim the ends of the boards, make it all neat and tidy. "Somethin' a bit fancy gets right to a gahrl," dad says. Walker apparently knows this too. Dad's standing below, holding the ladder so to make it steady.

O.K. I got to say, these two clowns are breaking every rule in the safety book. Not just a rule here and there, but *every* one of them. Kids, please don't try this at home.

Walker starts trimming the boards, and is doing a nice job of it. The off cuts fall to the ground, some with nails sticking out of them. It's time to move the ladder so Walker gets down, and he stands there with the running chainsaw, admiring his work while dad moves the ladder. Mid-move dad stops. He picks up one of his feet and a board comes up with it. He looks at Walker and smiles. Walker laughs and laughs. There's his flip-flopped foot with a board attached to it. Mom and Joan are aghast. Without the slightest flinch or look of concern, dad simply pulls the board from his foot, tosses it aside and goes back to resetting the ladder. I see the offending piece. The nail, and it's a rusty one at that must have penetrated dad's foot at least an inch, maybe two.

"Tetanus shot?" dad yells above the screaming chainsaw. "Yeah. I think I got one." He looks at us and grins. Mom covers her eyes and shakes her head.

She then looks at me. "If your father dies of blood poisoning…!" Sputter, sputter… It's of no use, and by now mom likely knows it. These two guys have flown around the globe together, they've landed aircraft on every remote corner of it through who knows what kinds of trying circumstances. To them, what they're doing is more fun than a barrel of monkeys, and stepping on a nail is just part of their amusement. Later, dad splashes some whiskey on it and calls it good.

The rain does come, a soft one that lasts all night. We have dinner with the Pierce's in the cottage and the roof does not leak. Walker and my dad are proud as peacocks, having protected their kin from the elements, and all.

Early next morning, there's barely any light, I hear someone rustling outside. I get up and poke my head out the door. It's dad making coffee. He looks at me and puts his finger to his lips. "Shsh…" It's fog outside, thick as pea soup. He puts his mouth right next to my ear. "Want to go out in the boat?" he whispers. I nod my head and withdraw it back into the camper. Mom's snoring away, I get dressed, put on a heavy sweatshirt and pull up the hood. I sneak out. Dad fixes me a mug of milk and coffee and we walk toward the lake. The wet grass brushing up against my bare legs is cold, cold. Very quietly we push the boat into the water and row out a ways. We have almost zero visibility. It's just us, the boat and the water, which is smooth as glass and quickly fades from sight into the mist. We sit and sip our coffees, we don't say a word. And then a loon calls, and then another, and another… until we are surrounded by the calls, the voices rise and fall and wither into space. In the dampness it seems they are right next to us. In our blindness we cannot tell.

Floating in this void we lose our orientation, we could be twenty feet or a mile from shore, we could be heading in any direction, and if not for sitting on seats, it would be hard to know which way is up.

The loons become quiet, there is a slight stir in the air and in only a moment the fog dissipates completely. Just like that, there is not even a hint it ever existed. Dad looks at me and smiles, we do not speak. Brilliant sunshine floods the scene. Our eyes adjust, thick stands of fir trees coming right to the water appear black. There is no sign of the loons, they have vanished, it could be they never existed. We are not far from the dock, and dad rows us back. Dad's nature is to be quiet, and so is mine. We do not talk about how mysterious this has been. Neither of us, I suppose, need to.

AFTERWORD

There are many, many more stories. The Nimrod got tired and mom and dad heard the siren song of a Starcraft pop-up camper. This rig had more refined accouterments; genuinely comfy beds, a heater, jazzy cabinets, and a solid roof. As nice as it was, without a canvas top, it wasn't the same as being in a tent. In time we (arguably) moved up again, to a fully enclosed and self contained Coachmen travel trailer. We continued to spend summers at Robie's, and took road trips; back to Canada a few times, and we explored the coast of Maine, discovering and falling in love with Mount Desert Island and Acadia National Park. And there were many more adventures fooling around with boats. Vic was off on her own with summer jobs and college, and I grew up. Somewhat.

Spending our summers in a tent created connections, to one another and to our world. And while having a low tolerance for four walls and fluorescent lighting may have its drawbacks, I'm O.K. with it.

GB

ACKNOWLEDGEMENTS

First, a heartfelt thank you to my readers. Thank you also to Sallie Bingham, Bill Bryson, Victoria Bunker, Kathleen Burch, Therese Desjardin, Patricia Erikson, Ken Kordich, and Bruce Reynolds for all their help and encouragement.

About the Author

Gordon Bunker has been described as a mild-mannered wild man and insatiable adventurer. His scribblings have appeared in *Drive, Roundel, Pilgrimage, BMW Motorcycle* and *Local Flavor* magazines, et al. His training as a writer is classical: go out and do life in the greatest breadth and depth possible. He has picked apples, built boats, cared for a public fine art collection, built and designed houses. And so on, this is the abridged version. Gordon once considered signing on with a commercial lobster fishing crew (the money was good). But he gave in to the fact he gets seasick just looking at an ocean-going vessel, thus proving he is capable of making a decision based on a practical consideration. Presently his day job is writer. So much for practical considerations. For fun, he regularly plays fast with the laws of physics on his motorcycle, has ridden coast to coast and border to border, and loves to hike in the mountains. Born and raised in the rock-ribbed hills of New Hampshire, he now makes his home in Santa Fe, New Mexico.

Made in the USA
San Bernardino, CA
22 November 2015